Ethical
Leadership

Robert J. Starratt

Ethical
Leadership

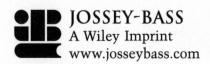
JOSSEY-BASS
A Wiley Imprint
www.josseybass.com

Published by Jossey-Bass
A Wiley Imprint
989 Market Street, San Francisco, CA 94103-1741   www.josseybass.com

Jossey-Bass books and products are available through most bookstores. To contact Jossey-Bass directly call our Customer Care Department within the U.S. at 800-956-7739, outside the U.S. at 317-572-3986, or fax 317-572-4002.

Jossey-Bass also publishes its books in a variety of electronic formats. Some content that appears in print may not be available in electronic books.

Library of Congress Cataloging-in-Publication Data
Starratt, Robert J.
  Ethical leadership / Robert J. Starratt. — 1st ed.
    p. cm. — (Jossey-Bass leadership library in education)
  Includes bibliographical references and index.
  ISBN 0-7879-6564-2 (alk. paper)
  1. Educational leadership—Moral and ethical aspects—United States. 2. School administrators—Professional ethics—United States. 3. School improvement programs—United States. I. Title. II. Series.
  LB2806.S664 2004
  174'.9371—dc22   2004003234

Printed in the United States of America
FIRST EDITION
PB Printing 10 9 8 7 6 5 4 3 2 1

Jossey-Bass Leadership Library in Education

To Jean, Irwin, and Diana,
models of moral educators

Contents

Tables and Figures

The Author

Robert J. Starratt, or Jerry, as his friends call him, has enjoyed a long career in education as a secondary school teacher of mathematics and English, as a principal of two secondary schools, as a professor of educational administration, and as a consultant to schools and networks of schools in the United States and a number of countries around the globe. His career as a student of education involved him in academic majors in philosophy, theology, and literature, as well as education and educational administration; those studies have been further deepened and expanded by the learning involved in his subsequent teaching, research, and consulting. His book with Tom Sergiovanni on instructional supervision, entitled *Supervision: A Redefinition*, is currently in its seventh edition, and his most recent publication, *Centering Educational Administration*, reflects the recent development of his scholarship on educational leadership and provides a bridge to some of his more recent work on the ethics of educational leadership.

Ethical
Leadership

Introduction

The current context of educational leadership presents a disturbing picture. Whether one looks at schools within a national context of legislated learning and underfunded programs (Lugg, Bulkley, Firestone, and Garner, 2002; Larson and Murtadha, 2002), an international context of the demands of the global knowledge society (Barber, 1996; Bottery, 2000; Fullan, 2003; Hargreaves, 2003), or an internal context of school systems responding to the imposed agenda of school reform (Goldring and Greenfield, 2002; Leithwood and Prestine, 2002; Oakes, Quartz, Ryan, and Lipton, 2000), educational leaders are challenged as never before. More is expected of schools without appreciably increased financial and other resource support. Demographic changes have brought additional demands to balance the needs of communities of varied cultures with an educational program of common learnings and common political ideals. High-stakes testing shrinks the vision of teachers to the technical dimensions of learning. In the simplistic public interpretation, educational achievement is equated with its standardized measurement (Foster, 2000).

While these challenges are daunting enough, they appear to be challenges to an institution whose intrinsic structures and institutional culture are taken too much at face value, as though the structures and culture themselves were not problematic. Thus, school leaders are called upon to accommodate these challenges coming from outside the school by making adjustments to their schools—increased use of computers; increased partnerships with parents; more multicultural texts in social studies and language arts; or the creation of inclusion classrooms, after-school programs, rubrics for assessments, or schools within schools—without seriously considering whether these adjustments will address the moral vacuum of the school that empties the work of students and teachers of its authenticity and significance. These adjustments will not change the consistent reality of most schools—that, despite the sincere efforts of many in these schools, the schooling process remains a huge waste of students' time and taxpayers' money, especially in the middle and secondary schools.

I say this out of a conviction that the learning achieved by students is generally superficial and largely decontextualized from student experience and the life of the community. In other words, it is inauthentic learning, superficial learning, fake learning, make-believe learning, rather than something that intrinsically adds value to students' lives and prepares them for responsible adulthood. Schools continue to go about the business of learning—the primary work of the school—as though it were simply or primarily an intellectual endeavor of absorbing prepackaged academic material, rather than a profoundly moral work that calls upon the full humanity of teachers and students for its realization (Buzzelli and Johnston, 2002; Foster, 1986; Hargreaves, 2003; Starratt, 2003).

After a while, students come to an increasingly ambivalent and disillusioned understanding that the learning required of them has to do with an academic body of knowledge "out there somewhere" that someone—this ambiguous thing called the state or the future or the job market or the adult world—requires them to study and figure out well enough to pass quizzes and tests, knowledge that is almost entirely removed from the realities they experience outside the school. Learning is reduced to getting the right answers to someone else's questions. There is little one could characterize as authentic about this learning. It is learning at a level of surviving the demands of school. It is learning how to appear to know what the teachers want you to know and demand that you know, not what you *want* to know or *need* to know or are *curious about* discovering. It is make-believe knowledge. Basically, schools and teachers are teaching youngsters to master the art of inauthentic learning, which amounts to schools teaching youngsters to be inauthentic. That's one of the reasons many school children resent the so-called bright students in their classes; either the bright students excel at being inauthentic, or they have been duped into believing the game of school learning is real, or really important. There is no sense for most students that they have to be responsible for what they know or that what they are learning in schools about the world has profound lessons to teach them about who they are and how to live a humanly fulfilling life or how they might respond to the challenges they are expected to face.

This is not to say that the curriculum being developed for youngsters to master is not capable of teaching these profound lessons. Rather, the instrumental approach to this curriculum demands that it be "mastered" for the "achievement" of high or passing scores on tests and thus eviscerates the curriculum of its moral content and the learning process of its moral character. For schools to deepen and amplify the way they promote learning as a moral enterprise (one that requires intelligence, to be sure, as well as a plenitude of other human virtues), they need leaders—both administrators and teachers—who themselves understand learning as a moral enterprise.

The work of educational leadership should be work that is simultaneously intellectual and moral; an activity characterized by a blend of human, professional, and civic concerns; a work of cultivating an environment for learning that is humanly fulfilling and socially responsible. In cultivating that environment, moral educational leaders enact the foundational virtues of responsibility, authenticity, and presence—the same virtues that should characterize students' learning. That is to say, the learning that is cultivated will itself be authentic, will be grounded in a fuller presence to what is being learned. Students will be responsible to what is learned and for the applications of that learning to their own lives. Thus, moral educational leadership is thoroughly contextualized by the core work of the school—learning—and the teaching that cultivates its richest and deepest appropriation and expression.

Part of the problem is that the issues that school leaders face tend to be presented and interpreted primarily as technical, rationalizable problems resolvable by technical, rational solutions. The human, civic, and moral challenges nested in many of those problems are not surfaced. Furthermore, many educators in leadership positions have had little or no formal exposure to ethical analysis or reflection; many lack a vocabulary to name moral issues; many lack an articulated moral landscape from which to generate a response. As Sergiovanni (1992) implies in his distinction between moral and managerial imperatives, technical expertise without a moral compass is inadequate for the task, as is a moral compass without technical expertise.

The moral challenges that schools confront are enormous. Nothing less than the quality of Western civic life and the international emergence of a coalition of democratic nations whose commitment to global social justice and mutual collaboration are at stake. School reform should be "more akin to a social movement intent on reinvigorating public life and reactivating citizenship than . . . to a technical reengineering of a corporation" (Oakes, Quartz, Ryan, and Lipton, 2000, p. 323). "Moral outrage about impoverishment has given way to technical debates about improvement. . . . In government, in teaching, and in teacher education, there has never been a greater need for social ingenuity and moral integrity" (Hargreaves, 2003, p. 203). Educators need to recognize "the serious limitations of failing to connect leadership theory and practice to broader critical and social issues such as economic deprivation and the chaos that deprivation creates in the lives of many children and their families" (Larson and Murtadha, 2002, p. 157). Clearly there is a call for moral leadership of schools.

This book addresses this situation, not by charting specific responses to the moral challenges educational leaders face (which I have attempted in a recent work [Starratt, 2003]) but rather by attempting to provide an intelligible framework for such responses. This framework deals primarily with foundational ethics that are focused particularly on the work of educational *leaders when they attempt to lead*.

Ethics and Morality

Ethics is a term that is used in a variety of ways for a variety of purposes. I use it here to denote a study of the underlying beliefs, assumptions, principles, and values that support a moral way of life. The product of that study is an ethics—a summary ordering of those principles, beliefs, assumptions, and values into a logical dynamic that characterizes the moral life. Ethicists attempt to bring intelligibility to and draw out the intrinsic logic of what constitutes a moral life—and, of course, what constitutes its opposite—and why. Therefore, I distinguish ethics from morality. Ethics is the study of what constitutes a moral life; an ethics is a summary, systematic statement of what is necessary to live a moral life. Morality is the living, the acting out of ethical beliefs and commitments. Often, characterizing leadership activity as moral and characterizing it as ethical mean the same thing: moral leadership involves the moral activity embedded in the conduct of leading; ethical leadership is the attempt to act from the principles, beliefs, assumptions, and values in the leader's espoused system of ethics.

One question that vexes both scholars and the public when the subject of ethics arises is "Whence is ethics derived?" Is ethics a set of principles rationally derived from a philosophical understanding of how the world works? Or is ethics a set of rules and principles that are explicitly or implicitly based on religious revelation and therefore presuppose belief in and practice motivated by that religious revelation? Is ethics a set of rules made up by religious or civil authorities to maintain the underlying power relationships in society? Or is ethics a set of norms that are constructed and chosen by members of a pluralistic, democratic society and that are considered pragmatic norms to guide the conduct of their public lives, norms that coincide with fundamental virtues that promote the fullest and deepest humanity of the community? Rather than a relativistic ethics in which everyone is free to decide for themselves, these are norms and virtues by which members of a community bind themselves to a moral way of living because they seem both reasonable and necessary to promote a richly human and civil public life.

The last view of ethics is the view favored here. This book is about applied ethics for a specific community of public servants. It offers them a perspective that might ground the moral exercise of their leadership. As such, the ethics of three foundational virtues are offered for consideration and for choice as pragmatically normative for educational leaders, not because they are grounded in natural law or holy writ but because they represent an appealing, a reasonable, and indeed an uplifting way to conduct business.

In reality, leaders do not start their day by asking, "How can I enact my core ethical principles today?" Rather, ethical principles are kept in a supply closet in one of the back rooms of our consciousness. They are maps that we consult only when the familiar terrain we are traversing becomes a tangle of underbrush with barely discernible and uncertain trails. In the course of a busy workweek involving budget adjustments, school district planning meetings, political negotiations with teacher union representatives, and reviews of building maintenance needs, educational leaders encounter certain situations that are challenging, not because of the technical problems they entail but because of the messy human problems or serious human consequences involved in the situation.

Alongside the technical aspects of the situation, the leader gradually shakes other pieces into a gestalt that reveals the moral challenge in the situation. That is when the leader goes back to his or her supply closet to consult the codes of ethics, the map with the large ethical topology (but not the details about the barely discernible trails in this particular situation), for guidance.

The Role of Leaders

Foster (1986) and Sergiovanni (1992) provided opportunities for the field to discuss school leadership as moral. Sergiovanni raised to a moral level such leadership issues as authenticity, stewardship, servant leadership, and responsibilities to other persons and to the school. While his book did not provide a formal analysis of the ethics of leadership, it pointed to the need for such an analysis. The recent work of Michael Fullan (2003) on the moral imperative of school leadership conveys both an urgency about the desperate need of schools for leadership and a view of moral leadership that is deeply passionate as well as intelligent in its commitment to transform the schools. His book is a happy sequel to Sergiovanni's work of a decade earlier, in that it will revive concern for the moral quality of leadership. Duignan (2003a, 2003b) has also been developing promising perspectives on moral leadership that connect authenticity and spirituality. Like Sergiovanni's earlier work, Fullan's and Duignan's work suggests the need for a fresh ethics for moral leadership.

In earlier works, I have referred to the ethic of care, the ethic of justice, and the ethic of critique as providing a multidimensional map of the ethical terrain (Starratt, 1991, 1994). Those three ethics are made up of basic assumptions about the way societies and organizations are or should be organized; beliefs about human beings; and central values and principles to guide choices, decisions, and actions. Langlois (2001, 2002) has used this three-dimensional ethical framework as an initial analytical lens to study the decision making of highly regarded superintendents in the province of Quebec, Canada. Her work led her into a deeper analysis of the decisions of these superintendents, one that revealed a profound engagement of their own humanity in the struggle to act responsibly in a situation (and therefore resist a superficially political and bureaucratic response). My own collaboration with Langlois (Langlois and Starratt, 2000, 2002) has stimulated some of the reflections in this book.

The body of scholarship in the field of public administration exemplified by the work of Terry Cooper (1991, 1998, 2001) brings many similar concerns about ethical administrative leadership into a helpful synergy with the ideas in this book. Cooper not only brings to the fore a concern for interpersonal ethics within the bureaucratic context but also highlights administrators' moral responsibility to transform bureaucratic and organizational structures so as to fulfill the mission of service espoused by public agencies seeking to operationalize democracy in civil society. This book shares a similar orientation, applied here to the organization of schools and the practice of education.

Unique among writers on moral educational leadership, Hodgkinson (1991) has attempted a more thoroughgoing analysis grounded in classical ethics going back to Aristotle, in the social psychology of organizational life, and in his own value theory. He presents educational leadership as a moral art in which the leader attempts to orchestrate the tensions among individual values, the core values intrinsic to the work of the school, and the value climate external to the school, both local and national, always insisting that the leader will never completely succeed in that orchestration. This book pushes the analysis toward a "virtue ethics" rather than the moral orchestration of competing values. It points to the work of leadership as involving the cultivation of virtues that will ground the work of the school as well as guide a diffusion of leadership among all the constituencies of the school.

About This Book

This book provides an ethical analysis of the virtues needed to infuse and energize the work of schools and hence the work of leaders in schools. Those virtues are responsibility, authenticity, and presence. Administrators, teachers, and students engage the work of the school as human beings, as learners and teachers, and as members of a civic community. These roles interpenetrate and enrich one another as the work of schooling progresses. Thus we treat the exercise of responsibility as a human being, as a learner or teacher, and as a member of the civic community; the exercise of authenticity as a human being, as a learner or teacher, and as a member of the civic community; and the exercise of presence as a human being, as a learner or teacher, and as a member of the civic community. The virtues of responsibility, authenticity, and presence interpenetrate and enrich one another. They need one another for their fullest exercise.

The book is intended for educators and for public bodies charged with governing and supporting education. Thus, it assumes that the readers of this book will need to go through their own learning process, a process of moving beyond the assumptions of technical efficiency in the delivery and performance of learning to an understanding of the learning process as a profoundly moral activity that should engage the full humanity of learners and their teachers. Similarly, their understanding of educational leadership needs to move beyond similar notions of technical efficiency to seeing it as a moral activity that engages the full humanity of the school community. The design and sequence of the book is intended to guide and illustrate this process of learning.

The book opens with a narrative about an educational leader struggling to clarify the moral task confronting him. It represents the struggles of many leaders trying to do the right thing inside the storm of state-mandated school reform. This morality play gradually peels back the layers of problematic notions about schooling to reveal the essentially moral character of teaching and learning and of a leadership that would support it. The reader is encouraged to wrestle with the moral challenges suggested by the narrative before moving on to the next three chapters. The middle three chapters provide a more formal ethical analysis of the foundational virtues of responsibility, authenticity, and presence. The fifth chapter returns to the struggle of the principal to probe the moral character of teaching and learning and to develop leadership responses that will move the school toward a gradual embracing of this moral character. Chapter Six suggests ways that university professors and school district personnel might use this book, either in graduate courses or in professional development seminars for educators.

Acknowledgments

Some words of thanks conclude this introduction. First I want to thank Professor Lyse Langlois of Laval University in Quebec for her groundbreaking empirical research on the ethical decision making of educational leaders. Collaboration with her has been a continual stimulus to compose this book. Andy Hargreaves, a recent arrival at my university, has been a huge source of encouragement in the carrying out of this work. Paul Begley, a codirector of the University Council on Educational Administration's Center for the Study of Ethics and Leadership, has provided steady and generous encouragement as well as conference venues for developing some of the ideas in this work.

A few words about the dedication: My sister Jean recently passed away. The event of her death led me to reflect on the quality of her character. She exemplified for me the virtues of authenticity and presence in our adult relationship and in her relationship with her children and her grandchildren. She represents the truth that mothers can be the most profound shapers of moral character in our world. Irwin Blumer and Diana Pullin are two colleagues at Boston

College, who in their unique ways have exemplified how responsible, authentic, and intensely present educators and human beings perform their deeply moral lives.

Finally, I owe a huge debt of gratitude to my wife and companion, Ruth, for providing the encouragement and the "family space" for the writing of this book. Many family projects were delayed and altered to allow my attention to the work involved in this book. I owe you, dear. Though I acknowledge my gratitude to these supporters, I am obviously the only one responsible for the final result.

April 2004   ROBERT J. STARRATT
Boston

1

Becoming Moral:
The Test of Leadership

I n order to catch the immediacy of a challenge to moral educational leadership, let us begin with a composite case drawn from
repeated accounts of actual principals and superintendents struggling with moral issues embedded in state and national school reform policies. The case presents a kind of morality play, a dramatic
art form of moral education in which you are asked to place yourself within the unfolding narrative and wrestle in your imagination
with the responsibilities that seem to be embedded in the situation.
I will suggest that you step out of the play from time to time to sort
through your reflections and gain some conceptual clarity about
your own moral landscape.

Al Auther, a thirty-six-year-old white man, is beginning the
third year of his first principalship at Roosevelt Middle School. He
has spent the first two years getting to know the school community
well, sizing up and making allies on the staff in the school district
office; reviewing student records; adapting curriculum and pedagogy
to accommodate state curriculum guidelines; reviewing the school's
performance against the guidelines of *Turning Points*, the national
blueprint for improving middle schools (Carnegie Council on
Adolescent Development, 1989), and attempting to identify the
major problems facing the school.

Al's school has a student population of 890 in grades five
through eight, with a decidedly multicultural mix of students.

Thirty percent of the students are lower-middle-class whites, most of whose parents have a high school education and are engaged in the service industry, the trades, or small business endeavors. Fourteen percent of the students are African American, many of whom come from what are locally referred to as "the projects"—public housing for low-income families and those on public assistance. Haitian American students make up an additional 7 percent of the student body, and Jamaican American students make up another 4 percent. Recent arrivals from Cambodia and Malaysia make up 5 and 4 percent, respectively; those from Brazil currently constitute 3 percent of the student body. The remainder of the students are grouped as Hispanics, although they can be broken down into subgroups: 18 percent Puerto Rican Americans, 6 percent Mexican Americans, 6 percent Dominican Americans, 3 percent Nicaraguan Americans. Almost all of the Puerto Rican American youngsters are bilingual when they enter middle school, although half of those students are academically on the margin due to frequent migrating between Puerto Rico and the mainland United States and changes of residences and school districts. Roughly half of the other Hispanic students have arrived in the United States within the last two years and have achieved varying levels of English proficiency. Some of the Haitian American students are bilingual when they arrive at middle school, and the Jamaican American students are normally quite proficient in English, having grown up in a former British colony. The Cambodian and Malaysian students appear to be struggling the most in their efforts to master English, especially conversational English. Furthermore, the Malaysian students are strict Muslims and tend to keep to themselves in their tightly knit community. Of the 890 students, 517 qualify for free lunches.

Fourteen percent of the student body is classified as having moderate to severe disabilities. Although the school practices inclusion of most of these students in a regular classroom, special education teachers still work primarily in pullout programs for specific academic assistance. Al has noticed that a disproportionate percentage of the students with moderate disabilities are African American and Mexican American students. He spoke with the special education teachers about reviewing some of their cases, but nothing has changed in one and a half years. He tried to provide some common planning time for the special education and general education teachers to talk about strategies for their special needs children, but they tended to retain a rather compartmentalized view of their responsibilities. Although some of the more severely challenged students have full-time teacher aides assigned to them, none of the aides has had any specialized professional training in dealing with specific disabilities. Neither, for that matter, have any of the general education teachers.

The school district, heavily dependent on state financial assistance because of the low tax base in the district, struggles to maintain a competitive teacher salary scale. Every year, however, young and promising teachers are lost to more affluent school communities, resulting in a relatively bifurcated teaching body of older teachers who have remained in the district and younger teachers right out of university, few of whom have come from diverse communities. Due to recent cutbacks in state assistance, the school system has had to enlarge the average class size from twenty-five to twenty-nine in order to maintain a balanced budget.

When Al Auther arrived as the new principal, his school was considered a low-performing school. Sixty-one percent of the student body was rated as failing or needing assistance on the language arts exam; 57 percent of the student body was rated as failing on the mathematics exam. The district had mandated that the school hold after-school and Saturday morning classes for those low-performing students. Those who needed still further assistance (students who failed the state tests a second time) were required to attend four weeks of summer school. However, the district staffed all of these remediation programs with volunteer teachers on a first come, first served basis. The veteran teachers, who were more familiar with how the system worked, tended to get these extra paying jobs.

The system provided these remediation teachers with no additional professional development that might help them diagnose specific areas in need of remediation or that might train them in alternative teaching or motivational strategies for underperforming students. The remediation classes averaged twenty-five students per class, and Al's visits to these classrooms revealed the same old, same old: teacher-directed pedagogy, worksheets, textbook-dominated instruction, and decontextualized curriculum units. Furthermore, Al had some evidence that many of the Mexican American students' difficulties stemmed from problems with the language of instruction and of the textbook. When he called these weaknesses in the remediation programs to the attention of the assistant superintendent for curriculum and instruction, he was shrugged off with the comment that the district had no additional professional development money available and that state funds for supporting these remediation programs were practically nonexistent.

The situation with special education students was even more desperate. Neither special education teachers nor general education teachers with inclusion students had received any professional development on how to prepare special needs children for the state exams. While the state made provisions for these students to have longer amounts of time to take the tests and, in some cases, have teachers interpret the questions for them, the funding needed to prepare special education and general education teachers for the basic work of mapping the instruction of special needs students to the state curriculum standards simply was not available. Al had asked the central office supervisor for special education whether additional funds could be squeezed from other parts of the district's budget for this purpose but was told by a sympathetic but frustrated veteran of the special education wars that she had already made that effort at several central office budget reviews. All of the district's professional development funds were being spent on workshops for general education teachers in order to map their pedagogy to the state curriculum standards for the general education population of students. Thus, the special education students as well as many of the second-language learners, who together made up the majority of those students at risk of failing the state exams, seemed to be denied, at least indirectly, a genuine opportunity to learn the material they were to be tested on.

During Al's first two years on the job, the school's record on the state exams had improved slightly, but the percentage of failing students hadn't changed, even though the raw scores of the failing students mirrored the slight improvement of the rest of the school. The school's improvement, however, was basically a reflection of the slight improvement of most schools in the state, a fact attributable, in all likelihood, to the increased familiarity of students and teachers with the testing protocols.

Al is growing increasingly uneasy with this situation. One of the provisions of the state policies on school reform stick in his mind. The state has said that the student accountability for passing high-stakes exams has to be matched by the school's provision of an adequate opportunity to learn the material they will be tested on. In other words, the state has said that it would be unfair to fail students on state tests and to penalize them for such failures by holding them back in the same grade or refusing to grant them a diploma if the schools have not provided these students with sufficient opportunity to learn the material needed to pass the test. The phrase, "opportunity to learn," however, has never been specifically defined, nor is there any special funding provision in the school reform law or implementation guidelines to ensure that all students have an equal opportunity to learn the material they will be tested on. When Al spoke to other principals in the district, they seemed to believe that the remedial classes and summer school classes were adequate mechanisms to ensure that students had sufficient opportunities to learn. They pointed to the improvement in student scores within the district. One of the veteran principals had commented: "We may not agree with the high-stakes testing policies, but it's not our responsibility to fix policy. Our job is to implement policy as best we can."

Reflection on the Case

How would you respond if you were the principal of Roosevelt Middle School? What would you define as your professional responsibilities in this situation? What would you define as your moral responsibilities in this situation? To further examine the issues raised in this exercise, after you have written down some of your initial responses to these questions, discuss them with a colleague to see how your thoughts compare with his or hers.

After this reflection, return to the narrative. Place yourself again in the role of the principal as he struggles to come to terms with the situation. You may or may not respond in real life the way you find the principal responding. You may want to write your initial responses in a notebook, paralleling the conversations and reflections that follow. On the other hand, you might want to let yourself identify with the character in the narrative, follow the train of thinking and feeling as the case continues to unfold, and later sort out where you would have diverged from Al.

The Play Continues

Al is increasingly bothered by his situation. There seems to be something immoral about punishing students who are failing the state tests, but he can't quite identify the nature of the problem. He decides to seek out Professor Margaret Wissen, one of the professors in the graduate program where he earned his master's degree in educational administration. He is fortunate to have kept up a friendship with her since he graduated, by attending yearly alumni gatherings and an occasional seminar the department conducts for alumni on leadership topics. He manages to set up an appointment with his former professor. What follows is a summary of how the conversation went.

Conversation with Professor Wissen

After exchanging pleasantries, Al explains his situation and his unease with it. Professor Wissen responds, "First, I'd like you to try to articulate your feelings about the situation. You need to clarify the sources of your unease, which may suggest something about why you feel that your leadership is at stake."

That suggestion leads Al to stumble through a somewhat labyrinthine explanation of a deep-seated unease about his responsibility to all of the students who are at risk of failing the state tests. As the principal, he is supposed to care for all of the children in the school, especially those whose life circumstances make success in their studies problematic. Al knows from his own school experience, as well as from his study of early adolescent development, that plenty of kids have the native ability to do well in school but for any number of reasons are not doing well and are unnecessarily punished in various ways by the school and by society for not doing well. Being judged lazy and uncooperative by authorities in schools only drives these youngsters to increased disengagement from their studies. As for special needs children, their handicapping condition often leads to unfair and culturally biased judgments about their intelligence. Most of the special education staff at the school are knowledgeable and caring professionals. They have been patiently working to unlock the learning potential in their students, but each child needs a carefully developed, individual education plan. The state tests, which many of the general education students are also failing, have so raised the bar for special needs children that some will only be able to succeed with carefully reconstructed curricula and pedagogies and testing accommodations for which no one in the district has expertise. Even that improvement might well fail to bring some of the more severely impaired students up to the passing score.

Al continues his halting scouring of his feelings and comes up against a strong reaction to this situation. "Yes! I can name it now: it is an *intolerable* situation. I simply cannot let this go on and face myself in the mirror and call myself an educator.

"Something deep inside me is at stake.

"On the other hand, what can I do? As principal, my hands are tied by budgetary limitations, by the legal obligations to implement the testing of the students, by the mandates of the superintendent and the school board to improve the test results. Other principals advised me on how to improve test results by putting our limited resources behind those students whose scores are closest to the passing mark. This, of course, would almost guarantee that the students most in need would not pass the test. That type of response is, well, so blatantly cynical; it violates my integrity as an educator."

Margaret Wissen responds: "Continue to probe what you mean by 'your responsibility.' Why are you responsible to these students at risk of failure?"

Al responds right away: "I'm an educator. I have a responsibility to see that my kids get a meaningful education—all of them, not just the smart ones. That's my profession and my promise to society, to these kids and their parents. That's why I went to university, to learn how to provide all kids with a meaningful education. I'm certified by the state to do just that. That's my professional responsibility!"

PROFESSOR WISSEN: Stay with that feeling about your professional responsibility. You are no longer a teacher. You are an administrator. You studied school administration and educational leadership with us.

AL: Okay, so I'm supposed to know how organizations work, how to change ineffective structural and cultural elements that will alter the directions of my school, how the various parts of the curriculum are aligned with state standards, how school culture locks people into seeing things one way, how our mental models victimize us. I'm supposed to understand something about a more sophisticated pedagogy that brings kids toward second-order thinking, that teaches for genuine understanding. Yes. And that's simply added to my frustration. The state testing policy places impossible expectations on our staff and most of the students. I don't know how to change this situation, yet I feel responsible for changing it.

PROFESSOR WISSEN: Okay, that's your professional responsibility. Anything else?

AL: Isn't that enough?

PROFESSOR WISSEN: No. Take a closer look at the kids. What do you see, and how do you feel about what you see?

Al slowly parades a line of students in his imagination, looking closely into their eyes. Many of them simply pass in front of his gaze as strangers, unknown and unrecognizable. Among the students he does recognize, he sees fear and also something like defiance and something like resilience. He senses a yearning and a hope in their tentative smiles. He sees the care with which their proud parents dress them.

He responds: "I see lots of kids whom I simply don't know. Others I see as real human beings, child humans who want a chance to grow up and taste life fully, express themselves, give and receive love, invent things, make useful and beautiful things. I see kids who want to be a somebody, not a nobody; kids who want to belong, to have a chance to participate in adult life. Among them I see human beings whose life paths will all too quickly branch off into dead ends, and I see others moving toward a broad expanse filled with possibilities. I guess I feel responsible to them as human beings, as one of them, and one of them in a position to turn them toward more promising possibilities."

PROFESSOR WISSEN: Stay with those images, Al. You seem to be saying that your responsibility is grounded in your humanity. You feel that your integrity as a human being is being challenged by the plight of the children in your school. Your sense of responsibility flows out of your instinctive response to the sacredness of other human beings. You are especially moved by the fragility of the young.

AL: Did I say that?

PROFESSOR WISSEN: More or less. That's an important foundation for articulating where your sense of moral obligation starts: our common fate, destiny, journey as human beings. We know that we have a basic responsibility to one another as human beings. That is often expressed negatively in the principle "Do no harm." Now, let's look at another part of the moral landscape you are exploring. What kind of an institution is your school? What purpose does it serve?

AL: I'm not sure I get you. If you mean that it's a public school, then its purpose is to serve public ends. I guess that means that the education kids receive is not just any kind of education, but an education pointing them toward and equipping them for adult responsibilities in society. And not just any kind of society, but a democratic society in the twenty-first century, a society that is undergoing the stresses and strains of unmet challenges at home and a messy journey of playing a part in some kind of new international political alignment. And that would mean preparing them to be good citizens and productive workers, and good parents and neighbors—stuff like that. Is that what you're getting at?

PROFESSOR WISSEN: Sounds like you remember *something* from your courses with us. Keep going with that train of thinking. If it serves public ends, to whom is it accountable?

AL: To the public, I guess, and to the public broadly conceived: those who elect the government, including the school board . . .

and those who make school policy and who hire school administrators.

PROFESSOR WISSEN: So what does that make you?

AL: A public servant?

PROFESSOR WISSEN: Okay. Are the kids in your school part of that public broadly conceived?

AL: Sure. I mean they technically are citizens with rights, as well as clients being served by this public institution.

PROFESSOR WISSEN: So . . . ?

AL: Well, that means that as citizens, children have rights under the law, and under the state and federal constitutions. That's where school law comes in. . . . I'm beginning to see where this is heading. You're suggesting that this situation might be ripe for a lawsuit?

PROFESSOR WISSEN: I don't think it is quite ripe at present, because the states have left the "opportunity to learn" condition vague and undefined. However, legal and political pressure might be applied to demand that they define the phrase. But what about you? Does this line of thought apply to you, to your position of leadership?

AL: I've already explored that angle. I'm legally responsible for executing the state testing policy. Failure to do this could result in my dismissal.

PROFESSOR WISSEN: Yet trying to fulfill this legal responsibility leaves you with a deep sense that this testing policy is morally intolerable for you to implement, at least as it applies to some second-language students and special needs children. Besides your sense of professional responsibility to these children and your sense of human responsibility, are you also able to ground your sense of responsibility in something else?

AL: If I lead a public institution, then I'm legally bound to protect the rights of children. Is that it?

PROFESSOR WISSEN: Do you belong to the public, broadly conceived, that the public schools serve?

AL: Yes. As a citizen I vote for the school board and other elected state and federal officials.

PROFESSOR WISSEN: In your role as school administrator, do you surrender your rights as a citizen?

AL: No. I can vote in school board elections. I guess I would feel some constraints about publicly criticizing a member of the school board in an election campaign and publicly supporting that member's opponent. That places me in an ambiguous position, though, doesn't it?

PROFESSOR WISSEN: Look beyond your rights to vote and your rights to support opposition candidates in school board elections. Look at your status as a citizen who also happens to be a public servant.

AL: Are you suggesting that as a public servant, I am somehow fulfilling my citizenship responsibilities in the work that I do? I've never looked at my work that way.

PROFESSOR WISSEN: Al, you are the state in action every day that you go to work. Think about that.

Look, I have to get ready for a department meeting in ten minutes. I think we need to continue our conversation. This has been a wonderful conversation. I'm proud of you, Al. You are looking beneath the surface of your job. Your concern about this opportunity-to-learn issue has hooked into something very central to who you are as a person and who you are as a professional. As you can see, you are wrestling with this, not only because it presents specific technical, administrative, and pedagogical challenges but also because you sense that some basic moral issues are embedded in the resolution of the situation. The moral disquiet you are experiencing won't go away, so you'll need to clarify and resolve that. Take some time to reflect on all that we have talked about, and look particularly into this last point, because I think you need to arrive at greater clarity about your role as a citizen–public servant. I'm going to loan you my copy of a book by Terry Cooper called *An Ethic of Citizenship for Public Administration*. I think it may be helpful.

Al thanks Professor Wissen for her help and agrees to see her at this time next week.

Further Reflection on the Case

Let's step back from the drama and look at the various responses of the players in the case: the assistant superintendent, the superintendent, the other principals in the district, and Professor Wissen. Can we say that the superintendent, the central office officials, and the district principals who were consulted see the implementation of the state testing policy as presenting any moral problems? Rather, it would appear that they all perceived that they have a political and legal obligation to implement the policy. That doesn't mean that they agree fully with its impact on all the students and teachers in the school system. Given the limited resources that the district has to devote to preparing students and teachers for the tests, they probably take the long view that things will get sorted out over time through the students' and teachers' growing familiarity with the tests, through year after year of gradually providing training for the staff in mapping their lessons to the state curriculum guidelines, through the gradual lowering of the passing score on the exam to accommodate the majority of students who otherwise, by being held back a grade, could paralyze the system or force it into bankruptcy. Their responses, in short, were to make the best accommodation to the state school reform policies that their limited political and financial resources and their administrative dexterity would allow. Their response was bureaucratic, legalistic, and pragmatic. They don't seem to have been disturbed by any moral misgivings about their roles and responsibilities. Their responsibilities were to provide services to the children of the community as efficiently as the resources provided them would allow.

Professor Wissen was very helpful. First, she encouraged Al to think through the feelings and intellectual contradictions he was experiencing. In so doing, she was signaling to the principal that the response had to emerge out of that reflection rather than simply be provided by the professor's expertise. She helped Al arrive at a clear judgment: "This is intolerable." This judgment of the situation enables Al to see that the situation is a moral challenge, a moral challenge to the principal as a professional who is responsible for cultivating the best learning environment possible for *all* the children, a moral challenge to the principal as a human being who is responsible for doing no harm to other human beings. Toward the end of the conversation, Professor Wissen pushed Al to explore another source of moral responsibility, something having to do with his role as a citizen-administrator, a principal who as a citizen was responsible for seeing that the public institution—the school—he was administering served the citizens in the ways the institution was intended to serve. The conversation ended before Al arrived at any clarity about this source of moral responsibility.

As you prepare to re-enter the drama, check your notes and reflect on your clarity about the issues so far.

Return to the Drama

Al is busy for the rest of the week. Besides a series of classroom supervisory cycles and budget committee meetings, he has promised his wife that he will help paint the upstairs bedrooms of their house on Wednesday and Thursday afternoons. Saturday provides the first opportunity for reflection on his conversation with Margaret Wissen, and for reading the Cooper book on the ethics of citizenship.

Al writes his reflections on the conversation of the previous Monday, then turns to the book by Terry Cooper, *An Ethic of Citizenship for Public Administration* (1991). As he reads through the book, he begins to see what Professor Wissen was driving at. Al paraphrases his insights from the text as follows:

- Citizenship carries with it an obligation to consider the well-being of the polity as a whole.
- The administrator of the public's business is not primarily a technician, not most essentially a specialist in some policy area. The most fundamental role of the public administrator is that of citizen. As a citizen, his or her specialty is the common good.
- The ethical identity of the public administrator should be that of the citizen who is employed "by us" and who works "for us"; a kind of professional citizen ordained to do the work that we, as part of a complex, large-scale political community, are unable to undertake ourselves. The public administrator is the state in action, the state the people want to work on their behalf and on behalf of the common good.
- The biggest issue for public administrators is legitimacy. Their legitimacy comes from the people whom they serve. They are instruments of self-governance by the people, with obligations to the people's well-being.
- The first obligation of the public administrator is to uphold the practice of citizenship, while the second obligation is to support and preserve the particular institution that he or she has been mandated by the citizenry to serve.
- Civic virtue of the modern sort involves free individuals who from time to time voluntarily forgo their self-interest for the common good. The public willingness of all citizens to uphold the common good is what guarantees the freedom of individuals to pursue their self-interest.

- The pursuit of self-interest takes place within a community. Self-interested individuals are dependent on a community to allow and support their pursuit of self-interest, for the common relationships within the community assure individuals that contracts will be honored, loyalties fulfilled, obligations carried out. The exercise of self-interest by free individuals depends on the virtue of everyone else in the community, and therefore it is in their interest to also be virtuous.

- The common good is the preservation of those common relationships that hold people together in bonds of trust, respect, and mutual affection, without which public freedoms become impossible, if not destructive of the community that supports them. Both individual autonomy and community are necessary for each other, and the fulfillment of either cannot be had without a common civic virtue committing the individual and the community to preserving the common relationships within the community.

- Moral responsibility is the element of character that maintains a link between the inner values of the individual and his or her specific commitments within the complex social life of the modern world. The moral person defines his or her identity by those values and translates the moral qualities of the self into specific choices in the role he or she is called on to perform in specific circumstances.

- Public administration that involves citizens in some form of coproduction of the work is better because it stimulates and supports community in the very production of the work. This kind of coproduction enhances the legitimacy and authority of the public administrator, because it is grounded in participation by and for the community.

As Al reviews his notes on Cooper's book, he can see more clearly the point that Professor Wissen was trying to clarify. His moral responsibility as principal of Roosevelt Middle School extends beyond the professional aspect of his position in the school to the common humanity he shares with his students and also to his civic responsibility to seek their common good as fellow citizens.

Al arrives the following Monday afternoon for the continuation of his conversation with Margaret Wissen. He thanks her for suggesting the Cooper book, telling her that it helped to open his eyes to a whole dimension of moral responsibility—the civic virtue required of the citizen-administrator—in his leadership role as principal.

PROFESSOR WISSEN: You wouldn't have understood the book if you weren't already wrestling with the issues. The answers were latent in your deeply felt unease. You just didn't have the vocabulary and the conceptual frameworks to name and organize the strands of your concerns and formulate a response to this situation. In our administration courses here, I don't think we do a very good job of addressing this lack of vocabulary and conceptual frameworks that would help our students address the deeper moral dimensions of situations they encounter on the job.

Let's see if we can summarize what you've managed to clarify for yourself. You began with a certain frustration that as an educator and an educational leader you could not find a way to respond to a situation that you intuitively understood as unjust. You came to see that the situation was not simply an unjust application of a policy, but an unjust policy. Your critique, therefore, was structural, for the policy disadvantaged not just this or that student, but whole groups of students whose life situations were not taken into account by the policy. It was like earlier policies or practices that disadvantaged women—not simply this or that woman, but all women—simply because they were women. The injustice of their situation was structural; therefore, the whole structural arrangement had to be critiqued. You see this testing policy as structurally flawed, too. It is unjust policy from an education perspective and unjust policy from a human perspective. And now you are seeing it as unjust from a civic perspective, because it ignores the need of some groups of students to achieve and enjoy the relationships within the democratic community that they are entitled to, the achievement of which are dependent on their school achievements.

AL: I wish I had a tape recorder so I could capture what you're saying. Your words are ringing bells inside of me.

PROFESSOR WISSEN: Well, good. Now, let's go back to your initial feeling of unease with the situation. You had a vague feeling of being obligated to respond to the situation, but you didn't see how to respond, especially after your initial requests for help from the district administrators led nowhere. We've begun to clarify some of the sources of your responsibility, but there are some unanswered questions remaining. Why, for example, did you intuitively respond this way, but other administrators did not? What was at stake for you if you did not find a way to respond?

AL: I don't know. I guess I've always had a sense of needing somehow to be true to myself. When I'm not true to myself, my gut tells me that I am taking the easy way out. I'm no different than anyone else in my ability to rationalize choices that I'm not entirely comfortable with. But I stay uncomfortable with those choices sometimes, because it's as though I've compromised an important part of who I am. Sometimes I end up not liking myself for the choices I make. And those experiences tell me to follow my gut the next time. Well, after a lot of experiences of dumb choices, your resolve to maintain some solid sense of integrity starts to strengthen; at least that's what seems to have happened to me.

When I took this job as principal, I wanted to make a difference in the lives of kids. That was a kind of personal mission for me. That was somehow connected to the fulfillment of who I want to be. I'm not going to be governor of this state or even, probably, a superintendent. Being a good principal, however, was something

I thought I could do. It would be my personal way of making a contribution—my way, however insignificant in the big picture, of making history. Wow, I'd better shut up before I get carried away. Does this make any sense to you?

PROFESSOR WISSEN: It makes a lot of sense to me. We rarely share these thoughts with one another, because we are easily embarrassed by appearing to be a goody-goody. What you seem to be saying is that you have developed a clearer picture of who you are, and you know it right away when you are true to that self and when you disappoint that self. I call that picture of who we are our sense of our authentic self. As we mature toward full adulthood, we learn from trial and error, from the way others respond to us and the way our own inner voice responds, that we want to be someone real, not someone fake, not someone who puts on an act for the audience. We experience ourselves as human beings filled with possibilities.

Becoming responsible is a growth process. Through the way we are raised at home, through our education in school, and through our interactions in the general culture, we are shaped to act according to approved patterns, for reasons provided by adults and other authorities. Gradually, though, we come to prefer to be more self-directed, less passive, more original than conventional, less a mimic of the culture than a person who enacts the culture. We become responsible by assuming responsibility. We assume responsibility for our humanity, for being and acting with others as the true "me."

We assume the responsibilities of citizenship by entering into our various social relationships responsibly, by respecting others for who they are and enabling them to be themselves.

When you took the principal's job, you assumed the responsibilities of the office, even though you had only a generalized notion of what they might be. Now you are much clearer about what those responsibilities might be. And you are exploring the idea of taking on the responsibilities of the job in a way that the job description hardly hinted at.

When you talked about your learning to be responsible and how your gut spoke to you when you were not true to yourself, you seemed to be referring to the two sides of moral responsibility. We are responsible, on the one hand, to avoid the bad, and your gut kept announcing that to you. On the other hand, we are also responsible to do the good. Being minimally responsible means we avoid doing the bad directly—directly causing harm to others. Being maximally responsible, however, means trying to do the good. Your initial efforts to deal with the testing policy was to prevent the harm it could do to two distinct groups of students. And you need to continue to do that. But you also need to look more at your leadership responsibility to do the good.

I listen to you and I get the sense of a person whose authenticity is on the line. Because you know who you are, you know that in this set of circumstances you have a moral responsibility. You have a responsibility to the kids, to be sure. But you also have a responsibility to yourself. To back off, to go with the flow would be a denial of your obligation to yourself to be the person you are. So let yourself recognize that. Be present to yourself being present to yourself. Appreciate who you are, and let that authentic self name your responsibilities in this situation. Let that authentic self energize your humanity, your professional instincts, and your civic virtue.

AL: I don't know what to say. I'm getting choked up with some very strong emotions right now. Your words have gone right through me . . . no, not through me, but to the center of me. Frankly, I feel afraid, because your words have suddenly placed me on a path I'm not sure I can handle or endure.

PROFESSOR WISSEN: I'm glad to hear that you belong to the human race. Those feelings are to be expected. But remember, it was your sense of authenticity that led you to follow where this situation was leading you. Trust yourself, Al. But realize that this sense of responsibility doesn't mean that you have to go out and fling yourself against the ramparts of injustice, impaling yourself in the process. You're a human being, not a world savior. You have certain things you may be able to do; you are working with a situation that may be amenable to modifications, perhaps not tomorrow morning, but over time. What you are responsible for is what is possible for you to do, you and all the others whose efforts you might enlist. Remember what Cooper says about coproduction of the services you are asked to administer. That may be the key to making an effective response to this situation.

AL: What would you suggest I do, then?

PROFESSOR WISSEN: I'd suggest that you go off by yourself for some further reflection. It doesn't have to be only the weekend when you do your serious reflection. That's part of doing your job, so you can do it during your work hours. The key to your responses will flow out of being fully present to the situation and all of its component parts—those you have identified and those that are more implicit in the situation. By being present, I mean bringing your authenticity right up close to the people involved in this—the kids, certainly, as well as their teachers, their parents, the superintendent and his staff, and the school board. Be present to the institutional constraints and possibilities in the situation, to the structures and process that get in the way, to the cultural attitudes that get in the way, to the political interests that need to be addressed. But be present to the deep ideals and values that may be latent in the situation, values and ideals that may be latent in many of the players in this drama. Most of the time we miss out on what is possible in challenging situations because we are not fully present to the people, the organizational levers of change, and the ideals and values already there in people waiting to be awakened and energized.

Al checks his watch and sees that he'll have to cut the conversation short in order to get home for an early dinner before parent-teacher conferences start in the evening. He thanks Professor Wissen for the great help she's giving him and asks whether they can continue the conversation the next week. They agree to meet the following Monday. As Al prepares to depart, Margaret Wissen again offers encouragement and suggests that Al continue to reflect on the issues during the week.

During the week, Al reviews his reading of Terry Cooper's book on the ethic of citizenship. He once again notes the point that Cooper makes about the public administrator's responsibility to the ultimate common good of the people, even while he or she pursues the specific common good that is served by the public institution he or she leads. Al chews on that thought: "So while you focus on the institutional common good that is served by schools—cultivating a high-quality learning environment—you should simultaneously promote the ultimate common good—sustaining and improving the relationships among the people that are essential for a democratic civil society. For me that means avoiding harming the teaching-learning situation through my administrative activity, as well as avoiding harming the relationships that bind the democratic community together. It seems that the high-stakes testing is harming both the ultimate common good and the institutional good of teaching and learning."

When Al meets with Margaret Wissen the following Monday, he begins with his review of Cooper's thinking and how that is convincing him that as a citizen as well as an educator, he has a responsibility to resist the harmful effects of the high-stakes testing agenda, especially on his second-language and special needs students.

PROFESSOR WISSEN: Well, let's put our thinking caps on again and get down to work. Let's focus more precisely on your commitment to be responsible. Last week we concluded that on a more minimal level, we are responsible for avoiding the bad, doing no harm. But we also agreed that especially for those who would lead, moral leadership was more about being responsible to do the good. As citizen-administrators, we are to seek the ultimate common good of the people—as you've just said, to sustain and promote the relationships that are essential to their functioning as a democratic community—even while we pursue the particular good that our public institution offers the people. Basically, the people of our commonwealth have said that education is a good that should be enjoyed by all the people, not just those who can afford to pay tutors or tuition for private schools. A free democratic society needs to have all of its people educated so that they can participate in the political and economic life of the community. That's an instance of distributive justice, in which a public good, education, is made equally available to all the citizens. As you suggest, the whole polity as well as individual groups suffer when equal opportunity to learn the common curriculum is denied to some. Okay so far? Is this more or less where we've arrived?

AL: Okay so far. This is really helpful. I'm amazed at how much clearer the issue is for me.

PROFESSOR WISSEN: Now we need to apply these general conclusions to the case at hand—students' opportunity to learn the material they will be tested on. What are some things that come to mind?

AL: Well, there is the problem that the tests don't test all of the things that are important for kids to learn.

PROFESSOR WISSEN: Can you elaborate on that?

AL: Well, if we are to teach kids how to be good citizens and how to be good human beings, as well as how to understand and serve the world, the tests don't test for the first two kinds of learning, and they don't even cover large parts of the third. The tests focus primarily on reading comprehension, writing skills, and mathematics comprehension. They implicitly test logical thinking, cognitive organization of arguments and explanations, problem solving, and the mastery of technical vocabulary. I'm not saying that these elements are unimportant. In many ways, they represent fundamental building blocks in constructing the intelligibility of the world. But the tests don't cover any of the important issues facing us today, nor do they touch on anything to do with human tragedies in history or any of the subtler forms of human courage in history . . .

PROFESSOR WISSEN: Let me interrupt you. I'm convinced; the tests are of limited use in assessing all that is actually taught and learned in your school. Yet student results on tests are publicized as the full measure of the school's work.

AL: Yes, and for me to acquiesce in that distortion is irresponsible.

PROFESSOR WISSEN: But let me ask you, do the tests provide *some* useful information?

AL: Yes, of course.

PROFESSOR WISSEN: And what are you doing with that information?

AL: That's part of what's bothering me. The information is being used to label some . . . no, *many* kids as failures. And they're not failures in my mind. They haven't had a fair chance to learn the material. We haven't had enough time, nor have we figured out how to teach the material in a variety of ways so that they can grasp it and use it to pass the test. For some of my kids, the tests themselves are problematic because they can't comprehend the language of the tests. Even if they know the answers, they may not have sufficient time to write their answers correctly, because they are translating their thinking into a language they are not comfortable with.

PROFESSOR WISSEN: Okay. These are arguments in support of your responsibility to do no harm. The tests actually harm some kids because they put these kids at an unfair disadvantage compared with the general education kids who belong to the dominant language community.

For the moment, put aside the issues about the harm that tests cause. I want you to look now at the proactive side of your responsibility: your responsibility to seek the good, to seek a higher level of excellence in the good that schools do. Look at the opportunity-to-learn issue from that perspective.

AL: Well, isn't my resisting harm something I can do pro-actively as a leader? As leaders we have to speak out against unfair policies.

PROFESSOR WISSEN: All right. Assume you are successful in resisting the imposition of the tests. No, rather let us say that you are successful in getting the state to hold off the high-stakes conse-quences of no promotion and no graduation. Let's say, even, that the state holds off on using the failing and passing categories and only reports the raw scores of the students' test results. That would relieve the harmful effects of the tests, wouldn't it?

AL: Sure . . . but the same kids would still be subjected to tests that only assess a fraction of what they have learned or to tests on material they had not yet had sufficient time to learn.

PROFESSOR WISSEN: Al, listen to me. I'm asking you to put aside your wanting to protect kids from being harmed by the tests. Look at the opportunity-to-learn issue from a different perspective. Has the opportunity-to-learn clause in the law made any difference in the way you lead your school?

AL: Well, . . . yes. It has alerted me to our collective responsi-bility as a staff to work harder with our underachieving kids. The problem is, the district isn't putting resources behind the effort.

PROFESSOR WISSEN: Look at *your* responsibility to do good. Address the opportunity-to-learn issue as your responsibility, as well as the district's. Be present to that.

AL: Hmmmm. . . . Oh! . . . Okay, I'm beginning to get it. I've been focusing on all the reasons why high-stakes testing is wrong, and then I blamed the district for not opposing the high-stakes con-sequences of the tests for special education and second-language

kids. And then I blamed the school board and the district officials
for not providing staff development resources. And I was doing next
to nothing myself to address my . . . no, *our* responsibility as well for
doing our part to improve their opportunity to learn. I was waiting
for someone else to solve a problem that I was at least partially
responsible for—responsible for through inaction, through not being
proactive and seeking to gather whatever resources we could muster.
Hmmm. We've got at least two special education teachers who have
been quite inventive in working with their kids. I could use them
as resources for the other teachers. And the Brazilian parents have
shown us some helpful ways to get parents from their community
together to work more closely with the school. There's probably
leadership in the parent community that we haven't begun to tap.
And there are probably lots of organizational arrangements,
changes in daily and weekly schedules that could be tried. . . .
Gosh, the moral leadership agenda was staring me right in the face,
and I didn't see it. How come?

PROFESSOR WISSEN: I suspect it's because we are socialized to
think of our moral responsibilities as avoiding being bad, like harming or hurting other people or breaking the rules. We tend not to
think of our responsibilities to do good, because that is so indefinite.
How do we know when we've done enough? Most of the time we
know when we've been bad because we've been raised to recognize
specific things as being bad. If we are raised in a racist or sexist environment, we do not see behaviors or attitudes that cause hurt and
harm to people who are racially different or of the opposite sex.
Now that we've been sensitized to the hurt that racist and sexist
behaviors and attitudes cause, we avoid them or at least suppress
them. But no one has taught us the opposite virtues, how to be
actively antiracist or antisexist—see, we don't even have words that
express such virtues positively. Perhaps *respect* or *empathy* or *caring*
could be applied, but we still don't know how to enact those verbs
appropriately because we haven't worked out all the tacit under-

standings and nuances of gesture and tone that one can assume in situations of familiarity. We have a ways to go before we are at ease with people of other races and with the opposite sex and they with us, due to the sorry history of our past relationships, the residue of which remains in significant ways in the present. When I read many of the cases used in textbooks about moral leadership, they deal with messes created because people in the cases have not been pro-actively seeking the good, seeking to create environments where the messes don't happen because the conditions that generate them have been removed and conditions that foster more humane and meaningful relationships are in place.

Another thing is that we tend not to think of our responsibility to do good in structural terms; rather, doing good is defined as how I relate to a specific person in a specific situation. The institutional arrangements are simply there; they define the institutional reali-ties. The leadership responsibility to do good clearly involves spe-cific interpersonal events, but it primarily means using institutional resources to improve opportunities, to open up new possibilities for people. When you were able to get past your responsibility of pre-venting harm to specific groups of students, you began to open up to your responsibility to do good, not simply by being nicer to these kids—although that is a good place to start—but by exploring how to use institutional resources to improve the good that schools are supposed to be providing—namely, quality learning for all kids. You began to see the issue as institutionally embedded; the moral lead-ership response is to make the institution more culturally respon-sive and more pedagogically inventive.

AL: Yes. . . . Yes! And you're suggesting that I should have seen the teachers' inability to be pedagogically inventive as a symptom of a larger institutional problem. Our institution is set up to privi-lege the dominant culture and to blame those of other cultures for their failures to adapt quickly. The curriculum is set up that way, the grading and promotion system is set up that way, the length of class periods, the semester assessments, the report card formats—they tacitly favor one group and punish other groups for not being adequately homogenized. I'm beginning to see that the opportunity-to-learn issue should have alerted me to the institutional arthritis that we have allowed to constrict our teaching and learning agenda, keeping it within familiar and comfortable pedagogies and organizational arrangements.

PROFESSOR WISSEN: Amen to that! We have the same problem at this university, Al. You are beginning to be present to this issue in a wholly new way, aren't you? Previously you were present to the issue from the perspective of your responsibility to do no harm. Now you are present to it from the perspective of your responsibility to do good. The problem is that from this perspective, you can imagine many possible institutional changes. Which is best, and how many changes should you make? Here is where you have to marry the virtue of responsibility with your civic virtue. There are many, many discretionary decisions in front of you. As an educator, as an educational leader, you're going to have plenty of ideas, some based on the research literature, some based on instinct. But . . .

AL: So this is where Cooper's notion of coproduction comes in, right? Because the school is a public institution that serves the people, I should find ways to involve the people in producing a response to the opportunity-to-learn issue. Maybe I should say *responses*, since the issue is so complex.

PROFESSOR WISSEN: Yes, good point. Think of the word *responsibility*. One way of interpreting the term is that it means response-ability—the ability to respond. That has two senses. One is the ability to respond to a judge who asks why you did such and such; your response reveals how culpable you are for your action. But the other sense refers to the ability to make a response to a moral challenge. Stay present to the issue from the perspective of the teachers and their responsibilities, the parents and their responsibilities, the students and their responsibilities, and the district authorities and their responsibilities.

AL: My mind is racing ahead now, and all kinds of possibilities are spilling out, like a waterfall.

PROFESSOR WISSEN: All right. Now it's time to slow down. You'll need to spend some time alone with a notepad. Write out all the ideas as they flow out, then look for patterns and organize them into some rational strategy. Then you'll have to subject your strategy to reality tests—those tough questions that the skeptics will pose. Then you'll have to look at whom you want to share these ideas with and how to structure some working groups. That's all in front of you. But for the moment, let's step back and look at how our conversation has been moving. Before, when you were focused primarily on your responsibility for doing no harm, you were blaming others for the problem. Once we turned toward your responsibility for doing good, what happened?

AL: I'm more in touch with myself as an educator. I'm generating ideas about teaching and learning. I'm doing more of what I think I know how to do. You were right to remind me about the human and civic aspects of learning, because I was falling into the pattern of thinking exclusively about learning the academic curriculum. I have to be more present to the human curriculum and to the civic curriculum, not only as important elements in their own right but as important contributors to and enrichers of the academic curriculum. By looking at the good I can do, I'm tapping much more into my sense of leadership. Talking in this way is more satisfying, although I'm also getting a sense of the huge task ahead of me.

PROFESSOR WISSEN: That's such an important lesson we have to learn—to keep looking at the good we can do. That's what we want to be responsible for. And, as you suggest, that's where we find ourselves.

AL: I'm going to need some time to absorb all of this. This conversation has been so helpful. I can't thank you enough.

PROFESSOR WISSEN: The conversation has been good for me as well. I think I've got some fresh ideas that need to be integrated into the content of my courses and into the discussions I have with other members of the faculty here. You are right to take some time to absorb this and to think your way through to some workable strategies. You don't have to come back to see me, because the answers to your questions are already out there in front of you. I'll be happy to continue to play your Socrates, but you soon may be so busy leading your school community that you won't have time for or even need my tiresome questions. You'll be getting educated through the feedback of the people and through the results of your leadership.

Analysis of the Conversation

As we step back out of the case, we should ask how it reveals, through the dialogue and reflection of the two parties, an emerging pattern of what might be called an ethics of responsibility. Can we also see a pattern that we might call an ethics of authenticity?

Write down your own reflections. If you were the principal, what would you have learned from the conversations with Professor Wissen? After you have engaged in your own analysis of the challenges Al faces, we will move on to a systematic ethical analysis in the next three chapters.

But what about Al? What does he do? He continues to find his way toward responsible educational leadership. We will return to Al in Chapter Five; you will be in a better position to appreciate his journey after reading the next three chapters.

2

Responsibility

When we first encountered Al Auther, the principal of Roosevelt Middle School, we saw his growing unease with state test results tied to the high-stakes sanctions of denying promotion and denying graduation. Al is dealing with a student population that is disadvantaged by poverty, by a lack of familiarity with the dominant language, and by a variety of disabilities, some of which may be incorrect labels assigned to students because of cultural differences rather than actual disabling conditions. Effective remediation efforts and the development of more responsive and effective pedagogies are clearly needed. Al is becoming aware that two of the school's subgroups are particularly at risk of failing the state exams: second-language learners and special needs students. There is a climate of blame and recriminations rather than an organized, systemwide resolve to address the entire situation in its complexity.

Al initially seeks additional financial resources to address the situation; he wants to provide more professional development programs for the teachers of these two groups, better remediation programs, and more time for students to learn the material they will be tested on. Al encounters several administrators who avoid taking responsibility for the situation, yet he feels obliged to oppose the harm being done to these students. The opportunity-to-learn

proviso in the law seems to demand a response. Al is having difficulty clarifying a professionally responsible solution to this harmful
situation, so he seeks help from one of his former professors.

Through Al's conversations with Professor Wissen, we see the
following process of clarification taking place.

- Names the problem: This is morally wrong, intolerable,
  harmful. The victims are being punished for the shortcomings of the system.

- Identifies responsibility for doing no harm: I have a
  responsibility to prevent this harm.

- Identifies the sources of his responsibility: I have responsibilities as a human being, as an educator, as an
  educational administrator, and as a citizen-administrator.

- Identifies what subjectively energizes the sense of
  responsibility: authenticity, the need to be true to self,
  to others, to the profession, to the role of citizen.

- Grows increasingly clear about responsibility: Al
  becomes present to the human, educational, and civic
  dimensions of the injustice. As Al becomes present
  to these dimensions and as these dimensions become
  present to him, they "talk back" to him, revealing the
  specific constraints and potential possibilities of the
  context, and challenge and invite him to be true to
  his self-concept as a human being, an educator, and a
  citizen-administrator.

- Gradually shifts attention from responsibility for
  doing no harm to positive, proactive responsibility:
  Al focuses on the responsibility of the principal to seek
  the specific good that his institution is intended to
  provide—quality learning for all children—as well as

the common good of healthy civic relationships among those in the community.

- Recognizes the proactive possibilities: The positive demands of moral leadership emerge. Al now sees that his moral leadership primarily involves the difficult but authentic work of pursuing the human, educational, and civic good of the students and teachers while responding to specific interpersonal, institutional, and political situations in order to prevent harm to students and teachers.

This review of the process of clarifying the moral challenges facing the principal in this case provides a convenient segue into a more formal analysis of the ethics that undergird moral educational leadership. In this chapter, we turn to a more formal exposition of the foundational ethics that are embedded in Al Auther's story. Remember that ethics is the analysis of what principles, beliefs, values, and virtues constitute a moral life. This chapter unpacks the intelligibility behind concepts of the foundational virtue of responsibility.

The Grammar of Responsibility

Most current scholars of the grammar of responsibility (Moran, 1996) observe that the term *responsibility* has two major orientations, or patterns. The first orientation enjoys an ancient heritage going back to the Hebrew scriptures (Brueggemann, 2001) and to Aristotle, Epicurus, Cicero, Augustine, Erasmus, Luther, as well as the later discussions of Hume, Kant, and Schopenhauer (Birnbacher, 2001). This orientation is what Jonsen (1968) refers to as the responsibility of attribution, the "holding responsible for the commission of an act" or what Birnbacher calls the ex post responsibility (*ex post,* from Latin, is usually expressed as *ex post facto,* which is translated as "after the fact," or, more loosely, "from the perspective of a past event"). By this, he means being held responsible for something one purportedly did in the past or having to *respond* to others about whether and why one did something. This orientation involves judging the morality or the legality of what a person did. The judging is done by those in authority or by the person himself or herself. It is a judgment that usually involves something considered bad. The ethics of such an orientation would establish what principles or values might have been violated and whether exonerating circumstances might have been present before or during the act. The "responsibility for doing no harm" of Principal Auther would involve this kind of ethical reasoning; the policy of high-stakes testing and its implementation would be defined as bad or harmful, and the principles and rules that were being violated by that bad activity would be identified. In this case, Al was passing judgment on the state policy, the school district that implemented the policy, and himself for carrying it out in the school.

In this first orientation, being responsible would mean responding to questions such as "Are you responsible for robbing that bank, defrauding your client, killing your spouse, cheating on the exam, or violating the terms of the contract?" by saying, "Yes, I did that. I own the act. I caused that to happen" or by saying, "Yes, I did that, but I was not aware at the time of the terrible consequences" or by saying, "No, I did not do that. I was there when it happened, but I did not do it" or even by saying, "Yes, I did that, but I was only following the explicit orders of my superiors. If I had disobeyed, I would have been punished." In all these instances, the person is responding to others by stating whether he or she was responsible for committing the act and what conditions or mitigating factors applied to the situation.

The second orientation is what Jonsen (1968) calls the appropriation of responsibility. Davis (2001) terms it the taking of responsibility, and Birnbacher (2001) calls it the ex ante responsibility.

(The usual Latin phrase is *ex ante facto*, translated as "before the fact," or, more loosely, as "from the antecedent perspective on the event or activity" or "from the perspective of expectations of future action.") This pattern of thinking about responsibility is concerned with a more general sense of expectations that in a given role, one will perform as a morally responsible agent. When one assumes the "responsibilities of office," one is expected to carry out the work of the organization (which usually is set forth only in general terms in the mission statement of the organization and perhaps in the job description). When one becomes a parent, one assumes the "responsibilities of parenthood," but what those responsibilities will be in any given situation is difficult or impossible to determine ahead of time. In both instances, antecedent responsibility assumes that the responsible person will have considerable discretion in making specific decisions. Besides discretion, antecedent responsibility assumes that the decisions will not be arbitrary but will involve due deliberation on the circumstances and the values that apply to the situation as well as caring for the persons who will be affected by the decisions. This antecedent responsibility is indeed a moral responsibility.

This second orientation toward responsibility came into use as a way to talk about the necessary moral stance required in the increasingly complex and multidimensional modern and postmodern world (Auhagen and Bierhoff, 2001b, Birnbacher, 2001; Cooper, 1998; Davis, 2001; Jonsen, 1968). In a more traditional world that is dominated by traditional definitions of ways to behave in almost all daily activities, one merely needs to obey the tradition. In the more complex modern world, where change and fluidity in social roles require greater improvisation and inventiveness, one is still held to be morally responsible, even though the rules have changed or disappeared or are vague or in conflict with one another. At the start of the twenty-first century, corporate financial fraud led to huge losses for investors when the companies went bankrupt. Managers claimed that they had not broken any laws or rules of accounting. They had simply devised an inventive way of moving money around and creatively naming accounts so that they could be listed as assets rather than liabilities. In the judgment of the public, however, they had recklessly engaged in high-risk ventures and intentionally misled investors and government regulators. In so doing, they failed in their responsibilities to the investors, to the financial community, and to the government. Through the wit of their high-priced lawyers, they might escape with minor jail sentences, but the public knows that what they did was morally wrong. It was a moral abuse of the "responsibilities of office."

This second orientation to responsibility is more recent in origin and development than the first orientation. English philosopher John Locke's *Two Treatises of Government* introduced responsibility as a civic virtue. That notion of civic responsibility took on an American character in the writings of Alexander Hamilton and James Madison in the *Federalist Papers* (Lerner, 2001). Max Weber (1958) broadened the term to apply to all aspects of life when he connected the Protestant ethic of responsibility with the "spirit of capitalism." He argued that wealth was seen as a sign of election by God for salvation. Being among the elect, successful burghers had to act accordingly. To legitimate their status, they had to be seen as exercising responsibility in many areas of public life—for example, by joining volunteer benevolent associations, serving on citizen committees, and supporting various charities (Davis, 2001).

Considerable importance has been attached to an ethic of responsibility by scholars such as Niebuhr (1963) and Jonsen (1968) within Christianity, Brueggemann (2001) and Vogel (2001) within the Jewish community, Cooper (1991, 1998, 2001) in public administration, and Moran (1996) in education. More recently, social science scholars (Auhagen and Bierhoff, 2001a, 2001c) have weighed in with research on the social phenomenon of responsibility as the human race faces the complex challenges of the third millennium.

The Responsible Educational Leader

Let's now examine how these perspectives cast light on the nature of educational leadership as moral work. An ethic of responsibility, especially the ex ante form, goes with the assumption of office in administrative leadership. Educational leaders must be morally responsible, not only in preventing and alleviating harm but also in a proactive sense of who the leader is, what the leader is responsible as, whom the leader is responsible to, and what the leader is responsible for.

Responsible As

Who is the educational leader? What is she or he to be responsible as? The educational leader is expected to be *responsible as* a human being, as an educator, as an administrative leader, and as a citizen-administrator.

As a *human being*, the leader is responsible for taking a stand with other human beings—not above them, as someone removed from the human condition, but as one sharing fully in it. That implies both an expectation of the best that humans are capable of and an acknowledgment of human limitations and failings. Al Auther was responsible in this way, empathizing with young human beings in his schools who were already facing obstacles because of various handicapping conditions or language barriers. Because he could empathize with them and their parents, he instinctively felt the injustice of the sanctions imposed on them by the state and local school system for failing the state exams. He was willing to stand with them in resisting this injustice. He also noticed the spontaneity and initiative shown by the parents of the Brazilian American students and thought he might appeal to them to help encourage some of the other parents to get more involved with the school.

Feeling responsible as a human being enables leaders to put themselves in another's shoes, to feel what they feel, to look at situations from their perspective. Al Auther was able to imagine the language difficulties that his recently arrived Mexican American students might have with the vocabulary and syntax of the questions on the state exams. Moreover, Al knew of the tug between being true to oneself and the pressure of peers to go along with the crowd, so he was likely to understand how his students got into trouble around the school through peer pressure. Aware of his own feet of clay, he could balance his role as disciplinarian with understanding and compassion and treat disciplinary situations therapeutically by imposing sanctions that would teach the virtue that had been violated. He could also understand the capacity of humans for generosity and altruism and appeal to that when delegating special responsibilities to students and teachers in order to help their peers.

Being responsible as a human being also implies that leaders understand that human fulfillment comes not only from work but also from family and friends and the cultivation of cultural and practical interests that also carry their own responsibilities and expectations. The leader, therefore, does not so totally focus on the work of the school as to ignore these other necessary components of a human life, for leaders and their families, staff and their families, and students and their families. Parties, musical and dramatic performances, socials, competitions, and celebrations should be a natural complement to the ongoing focus on academic learning.

As an *educator*, the leader is an educated person who continues to learn more about the human condition, about the social, political, cultural, and natural worlds that make up the curriculum the school intends to teach. The leader recognizes that education as a field continues to be enriched by research on learning; on child, adolescent, and adult development; on school redesign; on responsive pedagogies for various student populations; on authentic assessment strategies. The leader strives to read broadly in the educational literature and to stay abreast through seminars and professional conferences.

As an *administrative leader,* the leader studies the literature on administration and leadership, seeking helpful perspectives on school culture and school restructuring. The leader also seeks out other administrators in order to discuss difficult administrative dilemmas and challenges. In our morality play, we saw Al Auther probing for useful administrative solutions—budgetary relief, professional development initiatives, parental involvement, more critical assessment of the needs of those assigned to special education, and bureaucratic exemptions from the tests for special needs children.

As an *educational administrator,* the leader seeks to develop a comprehensive understanding of how the various dimensions and elements of the school work toward a harmonious and organic institutional unity (Senge, 1990), a unity that brings into focus the primary institutional mission of the school—quality learning for all children. Al Auther tried to keep up on developments in education by attending seminars for alumni at the university. He also had enough sense to seek help from Margaret Wissen when his nagging unease with the high-stakes testing situation told him that he needed to clarify his responsibilities. Certainly, educational leaders need to continue their education in ethical and moral understanding as they face increasingly complex issues.

As a *citizen-administrator,* the leader is responsible for promoting the mission that has been entrusted to him or her by the community to serve a particular common good—namely, the education of its future citizens. As a citizen-administrator, the leader also strives to keep in mind the ultimate common good of the civic community, which requires the leader to preserve and foster harmonious relationships within the community, especially among those subgroups that are struggling for acceptance in the larger pluralistic community. Al Auther intuitively placed himself within the civic community of his school district. He was at least minimally aware of the unequal power relationships in the community that were reflected in housing and employment patterns. He was minimally aware of the rights of students and their parents as citizens. By his own admission, he had not given much thought to that dimension of his moral leadership. He is just beginning to grasp that as a citizen-administrator, he carries citizenship responsibilities to ensure that the education of the youth in his school includes an education in civic responsibilities and in the cultivation of harmonious relationships among all the diverse cultural, class, and ethnic subgroups in the school. The quest for harmony, however, must acknowledge the necessity and desirability of conflict, for it is through conflict that the voices and the truth of cultural and ethnic identities are articulated and legitimated. In this way, plurality comes to be not only tolerated but revealed as vital to the humanity of the community.

Responsible To

Educational leaders are *responsible to* a variety of stakeholders: students, teaching staff, support staff, and parents, as well as district authorities, the school board, and the community at large. Let's start with responsibilities to students. The leader is responsible to students as human beings, responsible for upholding their inherent dignity as human persons, persons with human as well as civil rights. As young members of the human family, they should be recognized as a work in the making, as vulnerable and fragile, and therefore as requiring a secure and nurturing environment. Their young minds, imaginations, hearts, and characters need both direction and encouragement in their development. Since students' development is the primary work of the institution, their welfare should prevail over all other considerations in school decisions. Al Auther seemed quite clear on this point, even though the other principals in his district placed responsibilities to the state and the school board before their responsibility to students.

School leaders are responsible to their students as learners. This implies that leaders understand that the primary justification for all educational resource allocation should be its contribution to the learning of all students. In a time of budgetary cutbacks, school systems retain expensive football programs (large coaching staffs; cheerleaders and marching bands; stadium upkeep; team buses; and so on) and cut back on teaching and counseling staff, increase class sizes, cut library and curriculum supplies budgets, and substitute study halls for electives and enrichment classes. Budgetary constraints force difficult choices, but those choices should reflect clear priorities.

Furthermore, school leaders are responsible to students as young citizens who are in the process of learning how to be good citizens. Within the life and activities of the school, they have rights that must be respected and exercised; as citizens they also have responsibilities that must be learned and practiced in the school, as well as in the home and the neighborhood.

Leaders also have responsibilities to teachers as human beings, as learners, as professionals, and as citizens. As human beings, teachers should be treated with the dignity and respect that all human beings deserve, not as replaceable cogs in the wheels of a factory-like production process. Even as adults, they too are vulnerable and fragile and therefore need to be treated with compassion and encouragement (Blasé and Blasé, 2003). Administrators are considered exceptional when they habitually thank their teachers for doing a good job. That practice, while praiseworthy, should not be exceptional; it is the responsibility of all leaders to do that.

Leaders have a responsibility to teachers as learners. This implies that leaders will explore with teachers what their learning interests are, as well as what the teachers need to learn to help their students learn better. Since both theory and research indicate that teachers tend to learn better in teams, the responsible leader will explore teams as a basic format for encouraging teacher learning.

Teachers and support staff members are also citizens with rights and responsibilities, and leaders are responsible to them in this regard as well. Recruiting, hiring, and supervisory practices all need to respect teachers' and staff members' rights to fair and equitable treatment.

Leaders are also responsible to the parents and caregivers of the children in their school. As human beings and as citizens, parents and caregivers deserve to be treated with respect and dignity. Leaders have a special responsibility to see that parents who have recently immigrated to the United States, parents from impoverished backgrounds, and parents of special needs children have access to school staff, because these parents and their children tend to be at a disadvantage in the way schools are run.

Parents and teachers should be seen as important partners in the education of the young, but often teachers resist and resent administratively arranged partnerships. Many teachers disparage or patronize immigrant or welfare parents, believing that they have nothing to offer that would help in teaching their children. Many of these parents experience obstacles to attending parent-teacher meetings due to work schedules, language barriers, lack of baby-sitting, or cultural unease with public authorities. School leaders should see that partnerships with parents in supporting the learning of children in the school receive the sustained and sensitive attention that they require. Both childhood development theory and research on school-parent partnerships strongly document the dramatic influence that the social capital developed through such partnerships has on the learning of the young.

Leaders are responsible to their superiors in the school district. This is a two-way responsibility: one involves the responsibility of carrying out district policies with due diligence; the other involves the responsibility of bringing to the attention of district authorities the problems and unmet needs of various student constituencies. Both the school administrator and the district administrators have responsibilities to the parents, teachers, and students; thus, they should work as a team to carry out those responsibilities, each according to their office, within the constraints and capacities of the institution.

Leaders are also responsible to the local school council, to the district school board or other elected governing bodies of the schools, and to the communities they represent. Again, this should involve a two-way responsibility: one involves carrying out the policies and directives of the governing bodies; the other involves bringing before the governing bodies and the community, within appropriate communication channels, the unmet needs and challenges within the school.

Responsible For

In detailing educational leaders' responsibilities to various constituencies and stakeholders, we have begun to explore what the leader is *responsible for* in each case. The leader is not responsible for the students, for the teachers, for the parents, for the district officials, or for other stakeholders; they have to be responsible for themselves. The leader is responsible for developing and sustaining working relationships with students, teachers, parents, district officials, and other stakeholders. Specifically, as an educational leader, he or she is responsible for cultivating a caring and productive learning environment within the school for all the students. Cultivating a caring learning environment means insisting that teachers communicate genuine—not contrived—and continuing caring relationships with their students. Nel Noddings (1992) has elaborated on the necessary quality of caring in classrooms, a quality that can encompass challenge and rigor and strict accountability and indeed is vital to support them. Challenge, rigor, and accountability must be infused with caring for each child.

Authentic and Responsible Learning

The educator-leader has to be responsible for nurturing and sustaining a learning environment characterized by authenticity and responsibility. As Bonnet and Cuypers (2003) so convincingly argue, the school should devise learning activities that couple authenticity in learning with responsibility to and for the material students are learning. Here we touch on a very basic understanding of the responsible educator. In the next chapter, we will pursue the notion of authenticity in greater detail, but a brief treatment here will underscore how central authenticity in learning is to an educator's responsibility for creating a productive learning environment.

First, let us briefly address the meaning of authentic learning. Newmann and Associates (1996) have described authentic learning as requiring seven qualities or criteria. Authentic learning tasks ask students to

1. Organize, synthesize, interpret, explain, or evaluate complex information

2. Consider alternative solutions, strategies, perspectives, or points of view as they address a concept, a problem, or an issue

3. Use ideas, theories, or perspectives considered central to an academic or professional discipline

4. Use methods of inquiry, research, or communication characteristic of an academic or professional discipline

5. Elaborate on their understanding, explanations, or conclusions through extended writing, using analysis, theory, or argument

6. Address a concept, problem, or issue they are likely to encounter or have encountered in life beyond the classroom

7. Communicate their knowledge, present a product or performance, or take some action for an audience beyond the classroom

These seven qualities of authentic learning tasks point to a rich, multidimensional, committed kind of learning that engages the curriculum in its depth and complexity. This kind of learning goes well beyond simple recall of memorized information. The learner engages the intended curriculum in an intense dialogue, using a variety of investigative methodologies, sorting through various sources and types of evidence to identify an underlying pattern, structure, or significance. Authentic learning demands patient questioning, reflection, interrogating several potential explanations, and developing familiarity with several sides of a problem, question, or issue.

Authentic learning requires that the learner overcome bias, allowing the material to speak on its own terms, not forcing it into predetermined categories, not fabricating evidence that is not there. It requires respecting the integrity of the material under study, not making it out to be something that it isn't or something that conforms to an easy explanation. Furthermore, it is learning connected to something meaningful in the world outside the school, such that some people in the community will be genuinely interested in conversing with the student about whatever conclusions and proposals might have issued from the study.

This kind of learning is a far cry from much of the make-believe learning that still goes on in many schools, in which students are constantly trying to figure out what the teacher wants for an answer and offering their best guesses. When their answers are accepted as the right answers, they do not necessarily know why they are correct, nor do they care. The main thing is to avoid the public humiliation of looking dumb; "finding out what the teacher wants and doing it constitutes the primary duty of a pupil" (Wiles, 1983, p. 138). In such a learning environment, students have little if any intrinsic interest in the curriculum. The name of the game is to pretend you know what you're doing—just the opposite of authentic learning.

Authentic learning, on the other hand, carries with it a responsibility to what one is studying and for what one learns. As we saw in Newmann and Associates' seven criteria for authentic learning, the student has to attend very carefully to the material under study in order to uncover the real significance, underlying structure, or nature of relationships involved in the problem, question, or issue. In other words, the student cannot be irresponsible (careless, unfocused, inattentive, hasty) toward the material under study. The student has to attend closely, respecting the integrity of the material—that is, he or she must act responsibly toward the material, be responsible to its reality.

Moreover, the student involved in authentic learning has to be responsible for what he or she learns. What is learned may well have important implications for how the learner lives life or how the community conducts its business. An example of this kind of learning can be found in a sixth-grade science unit (Wiggins and McTighe, 1998). In this unit, students are asked to study the phenomenon of water and address three learning outcomes: (1) understand the composition and cycles of water; (2) understand and appreciate the extent to which water is a vital component of all organisms and the environment; and (3) understand their personal role in using and protecting the resource of water. Besides the expected learning tasks of discovering ways to make water and estimating how much water makes up plants, animals, and humans, students are asked to prepare presentations on the topic "If there were no water . . . " Two culminating performances of their learning require students to (1) engage in a debate on a use of water in which there is a conflict between industry and agriculture or between agriculture and environmentalists, and (2) create and carry out a plan for educating a specific group in the community about water conservation. In this example, not only does the learning conform to the qualities of authentic learning, but also the learning teaches youngsters how to take responsibility for using the learning in their own lives and in the life of the community.

Besides units in science, curriculum units in social studies, humanities, world languages and literature, and the arts carry important moral implications for personal and communal life. For example, a history unit on the Nuremburg trials after World War II teaches significant moral lessons about the limits imposed by the international community on the conduct of warfare. That historical event challenges students to examine their attitudes about warfare, about the rule of law, about racial and religious intolerance, and about the depth of cruelty and barbarism that humans are capable of (Starratt, 2003, p. 62). The lessons of history raise challenging questions for young and future citizens about supporting public policies that may facilitate or prevent other tragedies of history. In order for students to learn to take responsibility for what they are learning, they require a teaching and learning environment that reinforces the continual pursuit of such authentic learning.

Responsibility for Civic Learning

In the preceding examples, we have seen a clear linking of academic learning with citizenship learning, which is another area for which educational leaders are responsible. As a citizen-administrator, the educational leader is responsible for cultivating a learning community that embraces the learning and practice of civic responsibility. Such an environment would not only attend to the academic lessons about citizenship but also would include many developmentally appropriate ways for students to negotiate conflict as it arises in the cafeteria or on the playground, to develop appreciation of their own and other cultures, to exercise leadership within the student body, to engage in forms of self-government, and to participate in various forms of community service. To cultivate a learning community for the practice of civic virtue, the educational leader is also responsible for working with teachers and parents on projects to coproduce structures and procedures through which teachers' and parents' concerns can be heard and acted on.

Responsibility for the Organizational Patterns of the School

As Al Auther talked with Margaret Wissen, he began to see his responsibilities in a new light, as proactive responsibilities that included multiple possibilities (for example, redesigning the organization of the school, providing more time for learning the material to be tested when necessary, supporting more responsive teaching strategies, generating much greater parental involvement in the learning of their children). Because the school routines and organizational structures tend to define reality not only as it is but as it should be, these are areas of proactive moral responsibility that leaders especially need to attend to. Leaders need to take responsibility for being proactive, by which I mean that they need to shake off their inattention to what is staring them right in the face: the way that schools are organized simply does not work for many children (Barber, 1996; Hynds, 1997; Oakes, Quartz, Ryan, and Lipton, 2000). Many educators are only half aware of the obstacles that classroom schedules and structures such as tracking present to quality learning for many students. From many administrators, we hear the inexcusable response "Sorry, but that's out of my control. You have to learn to finish your work on time," as if the time allocation were a natural law rather than a human construct that harms some and advantages others. Educational leaders have a major responsibility for cultivating a rich, stimulating learning environment for all students, an environment that is flexible, responsive, encouraging, and diversified.

Responsibility for Quality Teaching

Besides the responsibility for cultivating an environment and a school organized for learning, educational leaders are responsible for quality teaching by all teachers. This is not to say that teachers themselves are not responsible for the quality of their teaching. School leaders, however, have a responsibility to continually cultivate quality teaching by providing abundant and varied professional development opportunities, by providing a stimulating supervisory system that engages teachers in deepening and broadening their craft, and by providing common time for reviewing student work in order to explore more responsive approaches to engaging underachieving students. Given the challenges in overcoming the institutional lethargy of well-worn routines, this cultivation may require vigorous tilling of the soil and weeding out of the chaff.

Mobilizing Adaptive Work

Ron Heifetz (1994) asserts that we need leaders who will challenge us to face problems for which there are no simple solutions—problems that require us to learn in new ways. Heifetz contrasts two types of leadership. A leader can influence the community to follow his or her vision, or a leader can influence a community to face its problems. He suggests that the second type of leadership—mobilizing people to tackle tough problems—is the leadership most consistent with our democratic traditions and the type most needed today.

Leadership is then seen as mobilizing adaptive work, which is understood as the learning required to address conflicts in the values people hold or to diminish the gap between the values people stand for and the reality they face. It involves getting people to clarify what matters most in a situation and what trade-offs they are willing to accept in order to address a problem head-on (Heifetz, 1994, pp. 20–27).

Schools are being challenged to accept a greater responsibility for all students. Clearly, one leadership challenge for Al Auther is to mobilize his teachers to tackle the problem of underachieving students, to clarify their own responsibility for finding ways to reach these students so that they will have a genuine opportunity for authentic learning. Linked to that is the responsibility for proposing and coproducing new school structures and processes that will further these opportunities. This is a tough problem with no easy solutions. As we will see in Chapter Five, the lack of authentic learning for these students is a symptom of a larger problem in the school.

The Higher Moral Standard for Leaders

Administrators who want to lead have to realize that they are called to a higher standard, something beyond keeping the ship afloat or making do with what they've got. To be sure, obsolete school buildings and equipment need to be upgraded, varied curriculum materials need to be purchased, and teachers' and support staff's salaries and benefits need improvement. All those things can be done, however, and schools can remain as dysfunctional as many of them currently are. Educational leaders are held to a higher moral standard of proactive responsibility for promoting quality learning for all students. Without a broad vision of what authentic learning is, administrators cannot lead, nor can they muster the moral passion needed to engage the school community in the arduous yet exhilarating work of making authentic learning a reality. The exercise of moral leadership will release the untapped energy in students, teachers, and parents, inspiring them to coproduce the changes that will support authentic learning for all of the students in their school.

Summary of Leaders' Responsibilities

In our construction of an ethics of responsibility, we have extracted some useful ideas and logical concepts from the messy and demanding experiences of school leaders. In contrast to taking the simple responsibility to avoid or prevent harm, taking the proactive responsibilities of educational leadership requires a more complex series of principles, as shown in Table 2.1.

The leader is responsible as a human being, as an educational leader, and as a citizen-administrator. The leader is responsible to all the students, to all the teachers, to all the parents, and to district officials and agencies governing the schools. When those responsibilities conflict, the leader has to seek the course of action that most benefits the students while taking into consideration his or her responsibilities to the other stakeholders. The leader is responsible for sustaining and developing a healthy environment for authentic learning and teaching, for democratic working relationships among administrators, teachers, parents, and school officials, and for promoting the learning and practice of civic virtues.

Table 2.1. Ethics of Responsibility for Educational Leaders

Educational Leaders' Proactive Responsibilities

Responsibility
- As a human being
- As an educational administrator
- As a citizen-administrator

Responsibility
- To students
- To teachers and support staff
- To parents
- To school district officials
- To state and local governing agencies

Responsibility
- For creating and sustaining authentic working relationships with all stakeholders
- For creating and sustaining a healthy organizational environment for teaching and learning for all students and teachers
- For creating and sustaining a healthy environment for the learning and practice of civic virtue for all students and teachers

We now turn to the question of where the awareness of these proactive responsibilities gets its moral weight. What is the internal moral logic, so to speak, that energizes or activates the acting out of the sense that one is morally responsible? For clues to that issue we turn to the next chapter and the virtue of authenticity.

3

Authenticity

In Chapter One, we saw in the struggle of Al Auther that his intuition of responsibility was connected with a deep sense of personal integrity, with a feeling that he was not being true to himself by shucking off responsibility for the plight of the second-language and special needs students. Robert Evans (1996) argues that leadership is much more a matter of who the leader is than how the leader applies leadership principles or adopts a leadership style. Real leaders are authentic. They bring themselves, including their deepest convictions, beliefs, and values, to their work. They are consistently themselves in their leadership activity. Sergiovanni (1992), Duignan and others (2003), and Fullan (2003) likewise cite authenticity as one of the primary characteristics of moral and ethical leaders. *Authentic* is an adjective, like *intelligent* or *effective*, that is often applied to leadership or to leaders without much elaboration, as though everyone in the audience knows what the term means. This chapter probes what the term *authentic* means and how it might apply to an essential virtue for educators—in other words, this chapter explores authenticity as a foundation for moral leadership.

An Ethics of Authenticity

What are the key ideas, central principles, and moral logic of an ethics of authenticity? The difficulty in articulating this ethic is that it is so foundational, so close to the bedrock of moral motivation that it is rarely analyzed in its essential elements. Psychologists have mined this vein much more than ethicists (Loader, 1997). Charles Taylor has perhaps provided the clearest philosophical analysis of this ethic. He suggests that there is a "certain way of being human that is *my* way. I am called upon to live my life in this way, and not in imitation of anyone else's" (Taylor, 1991, p. 28). There is a tacit moral imperative to be true to oneself. To not be true to oneself would be to miss the whole point of one's life. Since I am a unique being who will exist only once in the whole history of the universe, my originality is something that only I can discover, author, perform, define, and actualize. Only I can realize a potentiality that is solely my own. If I refuse this most basic human privilege and opportunity, then I violate my destiny and myself. I prostitute my eternally unique inheritance, my possibility. My possibility is like my child, the me to be born. I either bring it to birth—albeit gradually—or I gradually abort it. As Anton (2001) comments, authenticity is a matter of "how passionately one takes the whole of one's participations in a once-occurrent existence" (p. 155).

To bring myself to birth, however, is not solely my act. I bring myself to birth through others. My authenticity is ontologically relational (a point to be further elaborated below in the treatment of the ethics of presence). As Taylor says, "We define [our identity] always in dialogue with, sometimes in struggle against, the identities our significant others want to recognize in us" (1991, p. 33). Authenticity is also something I create through and with my culture. My culture provides not only a rich human language of self-expression and value through which I perform and define myself but also a storehouse of exemplars of virtue and vice who teach me the necessary moral lessons about life.

Here we are very close to the basic meaning of freedom. My authenticity is "grounded in a self-determining freedom" (Taylor, 1991, p. 39). My freedom to determine myself is seen within a culture that believes that there is something noble and courageous and inescapably decisive in giving shape to my life. What it means to be human is precisely to have this freedom and bear this burden, to enjoy this journey and brave its challenges. To be a human being in this sense requires a continuum of the most decisive moral choices.

We do not work out our authenticity in a closet or on a desert island. We shape our lives as unique human beings in a family, in neighborhoods, with friends. We recognize (re-cognize, that is, come to know again in a new light) ourselves in the dialogue that occurs between parent and child, between siblings, between friends. Loving relationships are crucial to our authenticity, for within them, we experience ourselves as lovable, as precious, as of great worth. For the infant, totally dependent on the mother, being alive means being loved. Withdrawal of that love is literally life-threatening. In the family, young children begin to learn the lesson that their freedom to be themselves is dependent on the tacit agreement that everyone in the family is free to be themselves as well. Somehow the family arranges its life so that everyone learns how to be free and at the same time limits the extent of that freedom in order to preserve the freedoms of the other members of the family. Rules about who gets to use the one bathroom in the morning first, second, third, or fourth provide a daily lesson in the communal exercise of freedom. The self-centered child gradually absorbs the lesson: mutuality is the way of the world; it is the way I can be assured of some exercise of my freedom; playing by the rules benefits everyone in the game (Youniss, 1981; Davidson and Youniss, 1995). This is true for individuals, for corporations, and for nations.

In the larger society, we begin to recognize that our freedom to perform ourselves depends on others allowing us the space and the resources to do that. It depends not simply on individual friends who support our freedom to be ourselves but on a whole society arranged to support this freedom. If I am to enjoy this freedom, then I have to grant a reciprocal freedom to others. Moreover, if we are to enjoy this freedom as a community and as a society, then we have to participate in the local and national politics of protecting these freedoms and join in the global struggle to sustain them. It is like children insisting that the offender follow the rules of the game, but now the game is much more complex and the effort to sustain the rules for the exercise of freedom is more difficult.

Bonnet and Cuypers (2003) offer a helpful analysis of the active and passive process of becoming an authentic person, using an argument originally developed by Taylor (1991). The active process involves constructing the self, sometimes even in opposition to societal and cultural rules and authorities. The passive process, equally influential in becoming an authentic person, involves attending to how others respond to our expressions of ourselves. The self appraises itself in terms of the feedback provided by the other. That feedback expresses either acceptance or rejection of the actively constructed self. Through the ongoing socialization process, youngsters hear evaluations of their words and actions as truthful or distorting, courageous or cowardly, appropriate or inappropriate. In this way, they learn how to negotiate relationships with parents, siblings, friends, and enemies within the unfolding drama of their self-construction (Becker, 1971). Moreover, Taylor posits the "larger horizon of significance" (1991, p. 66) as influencing both the self's and the others' definitions of meaning and significance. In the very activity of defining oneself, one uses the larger culture's meanings and values to articulate that definition or what in the culture one resists in that definition—for example, women and men may resist cultural and political definitions of themselves according to traditional gender and racial categories. As we will see, the active and passive sides of becoming an authentic person suggest a model for what will be proposed as authentic learning.

Connected to this basic human freedom to choose the shape of one's life is the notion that human beings share a basic dignity, simply because they are humans. Humans cannot be treated indifferently, as if they are gravel to be swept aside or parts of a machine that can be thrown away when they wear out. They have rights as human beings, rights that respect their inherent dignity. As citizens, too, their inherent dignity requires that they be treated civilly. Taylor (1991) points out that the framers of the Constitution of the United States recognized this crucial principle of human dignity. Everyone should have an equal chance to develop their own identity, however different from the norm. The founding fathers recognized the right of everyone to be different, but the value of difference was still grounded in the intrinsic dignity of all humans. Thus, sharing a common life that recognizes the legitimacy of differences brings with it the burden of sustaining the common life. Here Taylor links the ethics of authenticity with the ethics of social responsibility. Authenticity is grounded in community and in the activity of sustaining community. "Authenticity points us toward a more self-responsible form of life" (Taylor, 1991, p. 74).

Taylor understands authenticity as an ideal that draws us to raise our practice toward it. Thus, we resent societal trends toward greater manipulation, toward temporary functional relationships precisely because we have a sense of the ideal of authenticity. Politicians are no longer expected to be authentic; polls, not their convictions, dictate their strategies. Advertising is judged by its clever or cute punch lines rather than its truth. Corporate mergers that blur company loyalties and shuck off thousands of workers; for-profit hospitals, nursing homes, and schools; free agency for millionaire athletes; prenuptial property and asset contracts—all contribute to a general cynicism toward authenticity as a veneer for self-interest. Our cynicism is fueled by our intuition of the ideal. In Chapter One, Al Auther spoke of his unease with his choices to go along with the crowd; he intuitively knew that he was denying the ideal as it might be played out in his life.

Taylor makes a useful distinction between the *manner* of choosing to be authentic and the *content* of choosing to be authentic (1991, p. 82). Choosing the manner to be authentic, the expression of authenticity is clearly self-referential. Choosing an austere lifestyle, as did Dorothy Day, or an extravagant one, as has Elton John, is a way of expressing authenticity, a manner of being authentic. The content, however, of choosing to be authentic is always in relationship—relationship to a lover, to God, to a political cause, artistic creation, or career. Thus, Dorothy Day's authenticity was poured out in a lifetime of concern for social justice and for serving people at the bottom of society. Elton John's authenticity has been poured out in a lifetime of exploration and celebration of human feeling in music and through the charities he supports.

The confusion of manner with content is why authenticity is seen by many to be a license for self-indulgence. To claim authenticity as the justification for narcissistic self-preoccupation is to miss the point of freedom. Authenticity is the human challenge of connecting oneself to a wider whole, of finding one's life in dialogue with this wider whole, of discovering that the deepest character of all beings (a character revealed in contemporary physics, biology, and the humanities) is their relationality, their participation in the larger life around them (Anton, 2001; Bateson, 1979; Bohm, 1981).

Taylor admits that there will always be a struggle between the extremes of the best and the worst expressions of authenticity. Like democracy or pure love, authenticity is an ideal that can never be fully or permanently realized. Even persons who know what is at stake in choosing authenticity feel the attraction of going along, drifting with the crowd, zoning out, taking a holiday of self-absorbed indulgence. The ideal is always imperfectly realized, like a good school or a good marriage, like a good painting or a good film. A free society "will at the same time give us the highest forms of self-responsible moral initiative and dedication and, say, the worst form of pornography. . . . The nature of a free society is that it will always be the locus of a struggle between higher and lower forms of freedom" (Taylor, 1991, pp. 78, 79).

Nevertheless, someone in the audience might ask, "What about Adolf Hitler, what about Osama Bin Laden, what about Slobodan Milosevic? Weren't they authentic in the sense that they were consistently themselves? They brought their deepest values and beliefs to their work. What about characters in literature such as Macbeth, Ahab, and the Grand Inquisitor?"

To be sure, we can point to historical or fictional characters who were authentic in their tragic pursuit of a cause that visited death and destruction on other people. They were not fake. They were real. They thought they knew what their destiny called them to be. However, just as the mentally sick person who believes he is Napoleon may, in his sickness, be consistent in pursuing his illusions and therefore be considered authentically deranged, so too one may speak of people who are authentically evil, authentically mistaken, authentically deluded, or authentically infantile. Furthermore, no one is allowed to use immoral means to attain a moral end. Immoral means corrupt and compromise the moral end. This book treats of the virtue of authenticity, not authentic aberration. By the virtue of authenticity, I mean the healthy grounding of morality in a profound sense of the human vocation of being true to what one is, of being fully human. That means, of necessity, being in mutually affirming relationships with others. Thus, the authentic leader always acts with the good of others in view. Authentic leaders believe deeply in people and their abilities to make ordinary things into great things (Duignan, 2003a).

This objection, however, does force us to probe beyond Taylor's quasi-ontological base of "being oneself" as the bedrock ethic of authenticity. We need to supplement that with a more phenomenological probing of what authenticity means in everyday life to everyday people. What follows is not an actual account of what ordinary people might say. Rather it is my imagining of a situation in which I position myself at a bus stop where people are waiting patiently in line for a bus that is always five minutes late. I ask them, "What are authentic persons like? I am doing a study of what most people think about authentic persons." What follows is what I would expect to hear. The line at the bus stop is rather long, by the way, and populated equally by women and men from all walks of life, including a few intellectuals.

- An authentic person is real, not fake.

- They are not afraid to be themselves.

- They do not try to appear more than they are.

- I am at ease in their presence.

- They take me as I am.

- They do not lord it over other people.

- They let things be, accept the human condition.

- They respect who you are.

- They are not controlled by external trappings.

- They work from their insides.

- They look at why things are the way they are in people's lives.

- They attend to the little things that mean a lot to people.

- They tell the truth; they live the truth as they see it; they seek the truth.

- They seek to understand you, to see what life looks like from your perspective.

- They are there when you need them.

- They are not into what I would call the Hollywood heroics or the Madison Avenue hype.

- They don't impose themselves on you, yet they are open to you.

- The ordinary is important to them.

- They are not afraid to be vulnerable.

- They are not taken in by the glitz and glitter of our consumer society. They make do with simple things.

- They stay close to the common ground we all share.

- What you see is what you get.

- They find delight in simple things; they share that delight in simple things with you. When they are around, it's okay to stop pretending to be sophisticated and to likewise delight in simple things with them.

- Authentic persons disarm the powerful. They are not intimidated by power. They deal with the issues around which power may need to be exercised. For the authentic person, real power is the power that people who work together have to make good things happen or to oppose harmful things.

- Authentic persons are authentic with everyone: with aristocrats and paupers, with heroes and villains, with the powerful and the powerless, with extraordinary and ordinary folks. By that I mean that authentic persons deal with the human in all types of people.

- An authentic person seems to me to be a gentle person, a person who doesn't have to be anything in particular and who therefore doesn't need others to be anything in particular. So the authentic person invites authentic relationships that don't have to be prefabricated or pre-determined, just real, letting the relationship unfold gently and go forward or not go forward, or go forward for a while and then kind of slow down. As the Buddha said, anyway it goes is okay.

- Authentic persons are difficult to be around, because they quickly move beyond the surface impressions and superficial attractions and achievements where my life

is lived and engage *me*, not the image I try to project
to cover my insecurities and need for approval. That is
very unsettling, because then I have to try to be the me
that I am afraid to be.

- An authentic person is always trying to find what's real
  behind the appearances, whether the object is another
  person, an institution, a flower, a snake, or the law of
  gravity. Thoreau was that kind of person, perhaps
  aggressively so. He was always trying to get close to the
  bone of things, to what makes people and animals and
  nature tick. And he wasn't afraid to criticize the phony
  and fake.

The bus arrives and cuts off my interviews. I am sure that I
might have heard at least another dozen comments on authenticity that would have continued to nuance the meaning the term has
for people. Despite the intellectuality of the final comments, they
all seem to be circling around something deeply moral. Notice that
no one referred to an authentic criminal or an authentic cheat.
Notice also that while there was a clear uniqueness to be found
in authentic persons, there was a clear emphasis on the impact of
their authenticity on other people rather than on any extraordinary
talents and gifts they seemed to possess.

Thus, when we say that authentic persons are real, we mean that
they attempt to get at the insides of things, not to control or use
them but to dialogue with them as they really are. Of course, that
is a lifelong task because getting to the really real means peeling
back or penetrating layer after layer of the exterior complexity to
the simpler elements, which themselves are enormously complex in
their own microuniverse—as we have discovered, for example,
in the human genome project. Likewise, authentic persons come to
realize that about themselves: that their own authenticity is made
up of layers and layers of culturally and spiritually constructed
"stuff"—all those things that some recent philosophers point to in

their "deconstruction of the self." Oddly enough, however, authentic persons become more, not less, in the process of such deconstruction, as they become aware of where they came from, how they came to be. They discover in that process the much greater freedom to choose to be some or all of that self, including some or all of the culturally and spiritually constructed layers of themselves.

Awareness of the dialogical construction of the self keeps authentic persons humble and grateful and gracious: humble, because such self-knowledge points to how little they can really claim as their own achievement and as their own truth; grateful, because so much of the self is gifted in its development by the people who have cared and the lucky happenstance that enabled them to survive the illusions and the obstacles that might literally have killed them or psychologically or spiritually aborted their life; gracious, because they realize the fragility of the self and therefore how important it is to offer a gracious invitation of hospitality to the other, appreciating how such hospitality enables them in turn to make it through the day without anxieties about their own worth paralyzing their participation in the communities where they live and work.

Thus we see that authenticity as a virtue is always a relative achievement, always at risk, always in dialogue with the other in actualizing itself, always amplifying or diminishing in the face of daily circumstances. We also see how essential a virtue it is to living a moral life. One is tempted to say that the more authentic one is, the more moral will the whole tenor of one's life be in all its many daily activities.

We can conclude, therefore, that not only is the choice to be ourselves the most fundamental moral choice we daily make, but we can now appreciate how richly textured that choice is as it is acted out over years. The choice to be oneself is a choice to adventure into the real, the adventure of a lifetime, an adventure into discovery of who one is and who the other is and how the dialogue between the emerging real self and the emerging real other is both enormously gratifying and enormously humbling at the same time, because the real is all gift, not mine to possess, but mine to share and to share in.

The Ethics of Authenticity for Educational Leaders

The generalizations about authenticity in the preceding section, of course, apply to educational leaders as much as anyone else. First, let's focus on teacher-leaders since they are closer to the core work of the school, which is learning. Teachers are obliged to be true to themselves, true to their relationships, true to the nature of learning and the dignity of knowledge, and true to their civic responsibilities.

Authentic teachers are devoted to authentic knowledge. They appreciate a deep dimension of knowledge that implies an intimacy between the knower and the known (Sergiovanni and Starratt, 2002; Starratt, 2003). Authentic teachers understand that knowledge is a dialogue between the intelligences of learners and the intelligences found in the natural, social, and cultural worlds. Being in relationships with the natural, social, and cultural worlds implies involvement in and respect for those relationships. It implies many languages through which dialogue takes place. The knower and the known speak to each other, attract each other, puzzle each other, resist each other. There is no question of the knower living independently on some higher plane above the known. They are implicated in each other's existences. This holds for relationships of love and relationships of terror, relationships between humans and their possessions, relationships between humans and the HIV virus, relationships between jailers and prison inmates. Authentic teachers, in other words, understand knowledge from the standpoint of relationality.

The approach to the object of knowledge requires a profound respect for and sensitivity to its integrity. It requires the knower to be responsible to and for the known, for knowledge is not only a meeting of intelligences, it is a mating of intelligences and thus is a moral act. In the moral act of knowing, the knower accepts the responsibility of coming to know the known *carefully*—that is, full of care for the integrity of the known. This responsibility means putting aside one's sense of superiority and importance, leaving one's self-centered agenda aside, submitting oneself to the message of the known, willing to be humbled by the complexity of the known.

The work teachers and students engage together, the work of learning, also has an integrity that must become part of that working relationship. The teacher respects the struggle of a student to comprehend some parts of the curriculum. The teacher strives to grasp how students learn best by using a variety of sensory stimuli and imaginative approaches in teaching a lesson. The teacher refuses to accept an imperfect understanding of the material as "good enough." The daily struggle of an authentic teacher includes the effort to relate the curriculum to the lives of students, to bring out its significance to their current experiences and to the future demands that will be placed on them, and to appreciate, within the students' cultural and developmental growth, the complexity and ultimate privacy of the known.

Teachers' involvement with the agenda of learning is realized within the organizational constraints and possibilities of schools and their professional roles within schools. Max Weber asserted that modern organizations are simultaneously the greatest threat to human freedom and the major arena for its exercise (Eisenstadt, 1968). By that he meant that organizations impose a relentless discipline of interdependence and structured, predictable patterns of coordinated activity. No individual in an organization has the freedom to decide not to perform their prescribed duties, in order to "do their own thing." On the other hand, the coordinated resources of talented people and technologies enable people in the organization to do and produce things in one day that, by themselves, they could not do or produce in a lifetime on their own. So membership in organizations enables us to have a far greater impact on the world, for better or worse. Furthermore, a group of people in an organization can design a new procedure that enhances the effectiveness of the organization tenfold, or they may decide to break away and build a new organization that responds to different problems. Organizations, therefore, are arenas for freedom and creativity.

Likewise, schools as organizations impose a disciplined process of learning and interdependent structures for producing and enacting knowledge. Schools have class schedules and lab procedures that must be followed. In other words, schools constrain the freedom of teachers and students. On the other hand, teachers and students may address the complexities of learning by designing more user-friendly procedures and structures that enhance the learning process. Thus, authentic educators recognize the limits imposed by schooling but always test those limits in order to increase the quality, depth, and richness of the learning experience. For example, despite political and organizational constraints, educators continue to explore the use of more authentic forms of assessment because they believe in the benefits of more authentic learning (Hargreaves, Earl, Moore, and Manning, 2001).

Authentic educators exercise their authenticity in their relationships with other members of the staff, with their students, and with their students' parents or caregivers. Their authenticity is realized most certainly in their relationships with their students. This means that they work through the particulars of these authentic relationships every day in the classroom and around the school as they engage the students in the work of learning and demonstrating their learning. Authentic teachers know their students' names, their hobbies and interests, the neighborhoods they come from, and something about their family background. Authentic teachers challenge themselves to be real with each child and to invite, sometimes request, some level of authentic response from the student. The teacher's willingness to be fully present communicates a sense of respect for the dignity of each student.

When an educator becomes an educational administrator, he or she brings the sense of these authentic working relationships to the larger scope of administrative work and attempts to ensure that these become the norm throughout the school. The authentic educational leader will exhibit authenticity in his or her relationships with teachers, students, parents, and district officials. Despite the authority and power of his or her office, the leader insists on both the human respect and the civil respect that are the due of his or her colleagues. Extending respect to a colleague means listening carefully, discerning the needs behind the requests, and responding to the person, not just their organizational role. Keeping the mission of the school, especially the core work of authentic learning, uppermost in dealing with stakeholders and colleagues, the authentic leader works through the daily details required to live that mission. This steady linking of the mundane, everyday decisions to authentic learning for teachers and students provides a constant example of the leader's integrity. The work of the authentic leader involves the leader's deep commitments as a human being, as an educator, as an educational administrator, and as a citizen-administrator. The leader's identity is very much communicated in these commitments; it is the leader's way of being real in his or her working relationships (Loader, 1997).

Leaving the classroom for the principal's or assistant principal's office, however, can sometimes result in a forgetfulness that the primary work of the school goes on in the classroom, not in the principal's office. The research of Blasé and Blasé (2003) presents shocking evidence of principals who would not tolerate even the suspicion of strong teachers on the faculty who might attempt to exert leadership in the school. The power and privileges of the office may distort a leader's view of his or her identity. The leader is an administrator, with the power and authority to make weighty decisions, to be sure. But the leader cannot allow the ever-present administrative agenda to distract the leader from his or her authentic vocation; the leader is an educator, an *educational* administrator. He or she must remain an authentic educator, with a clear eye on promoting the learning of students, seeking ways that administrative decisions can further that work. The leader, then, must truly partner with the teachers continually to explore with them ways to raise the quality of learning for all children. Because most teachers need to develop improved strategies to reach underperforming students, the authentic educator in the leader will take special care of those students, not ceasing in the work with the teachers until those students reach the levels of quality learning that they are capable of. One of the reasons that underperforming students have difficulty with their schoolwork is that it seems too disconnected from their life, from the real world. In other words, they see the work of school learning as inauthentic work, work that is not connected to the shaping of their own lives (Meier, 1998). Until the school can answer the question "Why should I learn this stuff?" the work will seem like so much other nonsensical stuff that adults require of youngsters. Both the leader's and the teachers' authenticity as educators are at stake in this effort.

Recapitulation

What can we identify as the key ideas and principles and logic of the ethics of authenticity? First, authenticity is the vocation of every human being, the call to bring one's unique possibilities into realization. There is a fundamental moral imperative here. One either violates one's authenticity or chooses it. Second, authenticity is always relational, in dialogue with another, a cause, a career. Thus, while the manner of being authentic is self-referential, the content of authenticity is realized in relationships. One does not know who one is unless one can recognize oneself in the response of the other, and in that recognition choose to continue to be that kind of person. Third, one's freedom to choose and shape one's life is exercised in a society that guarantees, more or less, those freedoms for everyone.

The logic of the virtue of authenticity is that it obliges us to be true to ourselves and to our relationships at the same time that it obliges us to honor and preserve the rights of others to be true to themselves and to their relationships. The virtue of authenticity therefore has simultaneously a personal and a social moral dynamic. One cannot be sustained without the other.

Applying the virtue of authenticity to the work of education and educational leadership, we may say that the authentic educator is involved in authentic relationships with learners. Together, they are involved in the authentic work of learning and performing learning. In the process of authentic learning, they recognize their responsibility to honor and sustain the integrity of the activity of learning. That means avoiding inauthentic learning, such as plagiarizing someone else's work, memorizing information simply to recite it in class, not being able to point to implications or consequences in real life, or distorting the evidence to fit one's bias. The authentic educational leader cultivates and sustains an environment that promotes the work of authentic teaching and learning. Table 3.1 summarizes the ethics of authenticity for educational leaders.

Table 3.1. The Ethics of Authenticity for an Educational Leader

- Authenticity means being the author of one's life and the sole authority on it.

- Authenticity requires one to chose, in freedom, to be authentic; it is an ongoing moral imperative.

- Authenticity involves a person in reciprocal relationships. Reciprocity is an essential part of authenticity.

- Authenticity is exercised in a society that supports, more or less, the right of all members to an authentic life. Authenticity therefore requires participation in society in ways that support and sustain the exercise of authenticity by all.

- The authentic educator is involved in authentic relationships with learners. Together, they are involved in the authentic work of learning.

- The authentic educational leader unceasingly cultivates an environment that promotes the work of authentic teaching and learning.

As we saw in the case of Al Auther in Chapter One, getting clarity on the link between authenticity and responsibility is not automatic. Even the vague feeling that one's authenticity is on the line raises the question of what stimulates those feelings. How does one even become aware that one's integrity is at stake? The other principals in Al Auther's school system did not perceive that their moral integrity was at stake. Even after clarifying that awareness, Al was not aware of his proactive responsibilities. Figure 3.1 attempts to visualize these questions.

We in the audience sitting above the stage might begin to see a common logic behind being proactively responsible for creating a high-quality learning environment and being an authentic educational leader, now that we have listened in to the conversations between Al Auther and Margaret Wissen. However, the conversation had to wind and twist through the fog of Al's ambivalent feel-

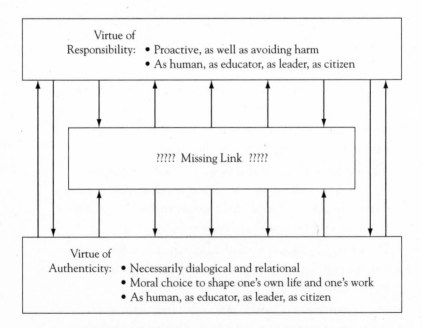

Figure 3.1. What Connects Responsibility to Authenticity?

ings and the underbrush of his partial understandings before the connection between the virtue of authenticity and the virtue of responsibility became clarified. Professor Wissen began to urge Al to "be present" to his situation, to "be present" to the students disadvantaged by high-stakes tests, to "be present" to teachers' responsibilities. In the next chapter, we will explore the concept of presence, and I will suggest that the virtue of presence is the link we are seeking, the link that connects the virtue of authenticity to the virtue of responsibility.

4

Presence

We have looked at the virtues of responsibility and authenticity as they apply to educational leadership. How are they connected? Is there something that ties them together, something that feeds and energizes them? In this chapter, we will explore the missing link between authenticity and responsibility: presence.

Humans are essentially relational beings (Taylor, 1991). We do not exist in a void, without people and society. We cannot define or express ourselves unless it is in relationship to others. We live in the actual or imagined presence of other people all the time (Mead, 1934). Our existence is perpetually dialogical. My presence to you brings you inside of me, and projects me inside of you. I am still me, although the me that I am is involved with you. You are still other than me, although you also reflect me to myself. The me you reflect back to me is either the me that I am trying or want to be, or it isn't. If it isn't, then I have to re-present myself to you. I have to try to be present in a clearer way so that you can take that me inside of you, be present to that me and reflect it back. I also have to be present to the real, authentic you, not a mistaken perception of you or my own a priori wish of what you should be. In being present to you, I project back to you my understanding of you. If that is the you you intend or want to be, then you affirm the perception of you that my presence communicates. If not, then you try a clearer projection of yourself, and so forth.

Being present takes place through the medium of language and also through our bodily expressions. As a university professor, I might approach an undergraduate who, as she becomes aware of my approaching presence, looks up at me with anxiety and apprehension. This response to my approaching presence tells me that she is reading me as somehow threatening. To set her at ease, I express a warm greeting and ask how she is doing. In other words, I try to be present to her as I want to be—a friendly, accepting person who simply wants to ask whether she has finished reading the book I loaned her three weeks ago because I need it for a project I'm working on. Because I have clarified my presence to her, she is able to respond with a relaxed smile and a thank-you for the book, which has proved helpful—thus reflecting back to me the self that I want to present to her. However, her initial response to me also set me to wondering whether my presence is occasionally threatening to students and whether I should avoid being present in that way.

This tiny vignette indicates how subtly our presence to one another creates a tacit internal dialogue that then issues in external expression. Being present implies a level of concentration and sensitivity to the signals the other sends out. Much of the time we have many things on our mind that keep us from being fully present. Often we are half present to the other, and thus allow the other to be only minimally present to us. Presence seems to be intrinsically dialogical. In the above instance of approaching the undergraduate, I might have just come from a faculty meeting where the usual malcontents had taken up much of the agenda squabbling over inconsequential matters. I might have been feeling frustration and annoyance from that meeting and let it show in my face as I approached the undergraduate, thus projecting a presence that, while it was me, was not the me I wanted to present to this student. In this instance, I was not fully present to the student, nor to the self I wanted to present to her.

Being fully present means being wide awake to what's in front of you. It could be another person, a passage in a book, a memorandum you are composing to the staff, a flower on your desk. Being present is like inviting a person or an event to communicate or reveal something of itself. We cannot be present to the other if the other is not present to us; the other's presence must somehow say, this is who I am, this is what I am feeling about this situation, this is the part of me that I want you to really consider right now. Being present means taking the other inside of yourself, looking at the other really closely, listening to the tone of the other, the body language of the other. This being present is also an unspoken message to the other that you are there, attending to the other's message, responding to the other from your own spontaneous authenticity. Being present means coming down from the balcony where you were indifferently watching your performance, engaging the other with your full attention, and risking the spontaneity of the moment to say something unrehearsed, something that responds to the authenticity of the other from your own authenticity.

This way of being present does not mean that you disregard the organizational context in which you and the other are embedded. Nor does it ignore the organizational roles you are called upon to act out. It does mean, nevertheless, that it is an exchange between human beings whose life spills beyond the boundaries of the organization and the roles they play, whose existence extends well beyond the organization, and whose rich humanity contributes to the fuller life of the organization. The risk of spontaneous exchange does not assume that the exchange is free from all boundaries. Rather, the exchange tacitly acknowledges organizational boundaries as well as societal and cultural boundaries but seeks within those constraints something genuine, something authentic between two human beings, so that their interaction, while subject to the artifice of all social exchange, is human work, something that provides some kind of pleasure and satisfaction and, at the same time, dignity and honor.

Presence enables us to look at the other and let the other speak to us. Frequently the other speaks to us only through surface appearances—a gesture, a look, a posture. But the surface also tells us something about the inside of the other. Whether the other is a plant or a bird or a building, the outside signals what is going on inside. A wilted plant wants water, a screeching bird wants me to stay away from her nest, a building's appearance tells me whether it is cared for or how the designer felt about the work that was going on in the building.

We are present to the other from a variety of perspectives. A medical doctor is present to a patient in a different way than a lawyer who is filing a case for injury. The doctor's presence is different from the spouse's presence by the bedside or the visiting chaplain's presence to the patient. Poets are present in a different way from politicians; psychologists are present in a different way from police officers. People are present as both who they are and the roles they perform; they are present to the other in the ways they read the language, posture, and gesture of the other as signaling what is going on inside. Professional people—architects, lawyers, doctors, sociologists, grammarians, literary critics, psychologists, biochemists, mathematicians, and airport security personnel—are trained to be present to the insides of things. They see the surface and discern the inner structures, processes, histories, aspirations, and values. In fact, being present is a form of knowing. But it is also a form of disclosing, of invitation, of communication and communion. Being present disposes one to act in response to the other, due to the knowledge communicated by mutual presence of one to the other.

Sometimes the other is much larger. Nelson Mandela and Bishop Desmond Tutu were present to the evil of apartheid and to the struggle for a free South Africa. They were present to the cruelties of the former regime, to the suffering of their people, to the institutional possibilities of existing government agencies. Their patient and persistent presence enabled them to exercise decisive leadership over the course of a painful transition to self-rule for the people of South Africa.

Presence, however, is not always benign. One can be present as a predator, an enemy, a contestant, a consumer, a user. These ways of being present convey a dominant relationship with the other or a desire to dominate the other. For the predator, the other is the victim of the predator's violence. For the enemy, the other is someone to be overcome, defeated, conquered. For the contestant, the other is someone or something over which, through the exercise of specialized skills, one gains a victory, at least temporarily. For the consumer, the other is something to be owned and used for whatever purposes the consumer decides on. For the user, the other is someone or something that serves a function for the user, and once that function is served, the user can toss the other onto the trash heap or walk away, leaving the other by the side of the road. Unfortunately, there is research evidence of principals acting in all of these ways toward their teachers (Blasé and Blasé, 2003).

You are present to something as who you are. If you are a bigot, you are present to someone whose presence for you is already distorted by your bigotry. A racist cannot see more than a stereotype in the other's presence; neither can a sexist or anyone strongly biased against particular groups of people. You are also present with your human history. Sometimes that presence involves ineradicable memories of sexual abuse in childhood, sometimes memories of a childhood in a loving family, sometimes memories of a lifetime of experiencing discrimination. How the other is present to you depends on your predisposition to be present to the other in a certain way, and your predisposition to allow the other to be present to you.

The Ethics of Presence

How does presence imply an ethical dynamic? First, presence can carry a hurtful intent or a threat of physical or psychological harm. From an ethical standpoint, those kinds of presence are morally repugnant, for they violate the human dignity of the other and the other's right to a minimum of public respect and civility.

One may also consider a more proactive presence that is intentionally dialogical, that brings the self into the eyes, the smile, the bow or handshake. This kind of presence communicates hospitality (Birnbaum, 1998); it offers the possibility of authentic relationship. It opens the door to the self and invites the other to approach the threshold. If this hospitable presence is reciprocated, then authentic dialogue begins. I am not necessarily implying a deep dialogue between close friends, although such hospitality may lead to that. Rather, I am referring to a simple friendly presence where the private self may be withheld, but the "real" person is nonetheless present to the other.

To be sure, many encounters during the day are purely functional: the bank teller depositing your checks into your account, the grocery clerk ringing up your purchases, the traffic officer waving you through. Even in these encounters, a thoughtful comment or gesture is entirely appropriate. Nevertheless, I am thinking more of the people we encounter every day in our work and in our neighborhood. Being more fully present to these people enables healthy relationships to develop, in which concerns about family, work, or politics can be shared; ideas can be tried out; or problems can be aired and questions debated. Does this being more fully present require something of us? It certainly does. It requires us to remove ourselves from the center of the universe. It requires a certain self-displacement, letting another person enter our space, then actively engaging that person in authentic conversation. Such proactive presence flows out of a tacit awareness that this is the way humans are supposed to treat one another, that this way of relating to one another is something that sets humans apart from everything else in the universe.

To be present to the throbbing life percolating all around us, to see people and situations in their complexity, to wrestle with what our common activity really means, to let ourselves be present to the pain and burdens of others, to get close to the beauty of those around us, to imagine the untapped potential in the person next to us—to be present to all that requires an attention, a sensitivity that is almost too challenging to bear. Yet when we become more present to all of this in our immediate environment, we find ourselves more alive, more connected to sources of life, more able to participate in this rich and complex life. Our presence enables others to recognize themselves in our presence to them. Our presence contributes to and enhances the human and natural energy in our surroundings. Our presence activates our authenticity and the authenticity of others. That is why this kind of presence is a virtue: it produces good.

The Link Between Responsibility and Authenticity

There is a fundamental link between the virtue of responsibility and the virtue of authenticity that activates the two and brings them into a dynamic relationship. It is the virtue of presence. In the absence of this virtue, a person's authenticity, no matter how well developed, may miss the leadership implications of events in his or her organizational setting. The sense of moral responsibility to respond to a certain situation or event grows in proportion to our being present to that situation or event. By being present to that situation or event, I bring myself to fuller attention. I bring not simply a disinterested curiosity, but myself, my whole self to confront what is going on. By allowing the fuller presence of the situation or event to speak to me, to be taken inside so that I can understand it, I can begin to discern what the situation or event asks of me. By bringing my fuller presence, I bring sensitivities that have been developed through education and experience; if I am a professional of some kind, I bring that expertise into the dialogue with the situation or event. If I am an authentic person, then the situation or event suggests a response that is consistent with the person I am, the values I embrace, the lessons I've learned, the commitments I've made.

In the case of Al Auther, the situation of second-language and special needs children in his school being punished by the high-stakes testing system was calling out for a response. The longer Al stayed present to their situation, the more the dialogue between his authenticity as an educator and the learning needs and possibilities of these youngsters was able to surface new possibilities not simply for modifying the testing situation but also for modifying and enriching the pedagogy employed for nurturing their learning. This example points to a significant characteristic of ethical presence—namely, that mutual presence can surface not only what is wrong or not working in a situation but also possibilities hitherto unseen or ignored. Not only do we grow to be present to who or where people are, but we grow to be open to who they can become and where they might journey. Presence to their possibilities leads to a response of invitation: Is this who you want to be? Is this where you want to go with this situation? Then let us explore together how we might get there. That exploration is precisely the proactive responsibility of the leader. The proactively responsible leader goes beyond tinkering with the status quo to a clearer sense of what it will take to transform the status quo into something more humanly fulfilling that also more thoroughly fulfills the mission of the organization.

Types of Presence

As with responsibility, there are two sides to the morality of presence. That is, we are under an implicit moral imperative to be present to the people and things around us. Being half present can easily be the cause of harm to another, whether we are driving a car, making a joke, making love, keeping accounts, or teaching. We have a responsibility to avoid being half present. There is also an ex ante sense in which being present is expected of us if we are to be authentic and if we are to be responsible. Being present enables us to be authentic and to be responsible. There are three ways of being present that suggest an ethical dynamic for educational leaders: an affirming presence, a critical presence, and an enabling presence.

Affirming Presence

Affirming presence involves foregrounding an attitude of unconditional regard for the person or persons you are working with. It means not only holding them interiorly in high regard but also explicitly expressing your regard in a variety of ways. In Anglo-Saxon cultures, most people favor understatement rather than overstatement in this area: a brief compliment, a thank-you, a word of concern when the situation calls for it; other cultures require more visible enthusiasm. More than anything, the message will be picked up quite clearly from the leader's actions. Those actions will communicate the following unequivocal messages: no one in the school can be used as a means to an end; every person enjoys an intrinsic dignity and worth; we expect people to reach out and help one another here; we believe that every person has an abundance of talents and good ideas and, given some encouragement, will enrich the life of the community.

Affirming presence communicates the message that others have the right to be who they are. During formal and informal gatherings, others are invited to express their authentic individuality and to bring all the talents of that individuality to the life of the school. In the process of extending that invitation, perhaps through understatement and a subtle progression of shared confidences, the leader reveals his or her human side as well. In the course of discussing ideas and interests, the leader reveals the strong belief that the primary work of the school—student learning—is enriched by a plurality of talents, interests, and backgrounds among both students and teachers. The work of learning will be different for each child because of the unique life history that child brings to the task. But that work of learning is a public work as well, a work that is deepened and broadened by the multiple perspectives that different teachers and different students bring.

The work of learning provides the underlying institutional context for an affirming presence. The school is not a social club where people gather for companionship and recreation. The school, instead, is a public institution serving the community, with a mission of educating all children to the best that their ability allows. Thus, the affirming presence of the leader is an affirmation in the context of the common commitment of the community to work together to promote a quality learning environment for all of the students. As was mentioned above, however, the leader is present not only to a surface understanding of learning—the memorization of information, the application of mathematical formulas to word problems, remembering the correct spelling of big words, applying the correct measurements in lab science—but even more to the transformative impact of authentic learning. That vision of learning gives a depth and richness to the mission of the school by proposing the exciting possibilities of learning in order to free youngsters from the narrow confines of parochial and biased views of their natural, cultural, and social worlds. In other words, every day, the leader affirms with the teachers the transforming possibilities embedded in the students' encounter with the curriculum. The teachers, in turn, call out to the students through their affirming presence: look at the fascinating stuff about our world that we will be dealing with today! Within that mission of promoting authentic, transformative learning, teachers, counselors, students, parents, nurses, social workers, custodians, secretaries, bus drivers, cafeteria workers, and others bring their human talents and skills to the work.

These workers, however, are not robots, each performing a preprogrammed function. They are human beings engaged in very risky work, the daily work of overcoming ignorance and confusion and obsolete understandings. It is risky work because, in the process, fragile human beings may be exposed to embarrassment, ridicule, and humiliation in the public forum of the classroom as they strug-gle to grasp what the teacher and the curriculum is asking of them. For teachers still mastering their craft, there is the risky business of looking like a bungler in front of the principal who is visiting their classroom or bringing a parent's complaint to their attention. The institutional context of the work of learning carries intrinsically moral overtones (Starratt, 2003). The school schedule, classroom and playground rules, reward systems, corridor displays, home-school communications—all should express an affirming institutional pres-ence. The work of learning demands such an affirming presence if it is to flourish as *human work*.

Within such an educating community, everyone is affirmed; the metaphor of family is invoked; celebrations of achievement are vis-ible all around the school; photographs of teams of teachers and teams of students involved in a variety of projects adorn the school bulletin boards. When people in the school are present to one another, even on bad days, there is clear evidence of respect, humor, sharing of ideas and criticisms; there are shouted greetings and plenty of exclamations of "thank-you," "good work!" and "we need to talk about that."

Almost always, the affirming presence of the school leader gen-erates an affirming presence among the staff and students. However, the affirming leader will also attempt to build structures, processes, and rituals within the school week, month, or semester that will allow members of the school family to affirm one another and de-velop a strong sense of community. Sometimes such community building involves creating a more formally structured process for communicating with parents; sometimes a student forum for airing grievances and resolving conflict between groups within the school; sometimes a series of sharing sessions with the officers of the teach-ers union; sometimes a faculty musical depicting the foibles of the adults in the school. However those rituals are formalized, one thing will be constant: the visible presence of the leader throughout the building, greeting staff and students, encouraging, cheerleading, supporting, and consoling.

Critical Presence

We have seen how we can encounter another—a person, a group, a situation, an institution, or an institutional policy or practice—whose presence is not benign, who is not open to a dialogue of mutual affirmation and respect, or who asks us to respond in ways that would violate our authenticity and our responsibilities. We encounter presences that are predatory, manipulative, bigoted, controlling, or domineering (Blasé and Blasé, 2003). We sense a threat to who we know we are through the distorted reflection of ourselves that the other's presence reflects back to us. This awareness causes us to withdraw, resist, or respond with a candid reflection back to the other about our perceptions of the other's presence. The other may recognize the problem and change the way he or she is present to us. If the other does not change his or her presence to us, we can respond with resistance or withdrawal, depending on our perception of what is at stake.

Sometimes we sense anger or resentment in the other's presence. Our presence to this anger and resentment triggers a reflection on ourselves and how we may have recently acted toward this person or group. Sometimes that reflection reveals a recent episode in which we criticized some project they had been involved with. Sometimes that reflection reveals a pattern of our not listening, of being distant and half present to that person or group. Sometimes that reflection will reveal a more generalized resentment of us as white, as male, as an administrator, or as a representative of an institution that has treated this person or group badly. Sometimes that reflection will reveal nothing particular that might be the cause of that angry and resentful presence of the other. It is possible that the anger and resentment is a carryover from something that did not involve us at all—a fight with a spouse, a frustrating day in class, or the usurpation of the person's favorite parking space. For communication to be opened up in all of these cases, we need to respond to that presence by candidly reflecting back to that other that we are sensing something like anger or resentment in the other's presence to us and we want to check to see whether that perception is accurate, and if so, to understand what is causing the anger. When the person or group senses your willingness to listen, they have an opportunity to be more authentically present to you by getting the source of anger off their chest, anger over something that has offended their own authenticity in some way.

We can say, then, that a critical presence in an encounter with the other can work in both directions, resulting either in a critical appraisal of oneself as the cause of a blockage to authentic communication because of some real or perceived harm one has visited on the other, or in a critical appraisal of something in the other's presence that blocks our mutual ability to communicate authentically.

In the case of Al Auther, there seemed to be a double-edged critical presence to the situation of high-stakes testing. On one hand, Al Auther was present to an institutional practice that was structurally unjust, because it placed second-language and special needs children at a distinct disadvantage and then punished them for not overcoming that disadvantage despite little or no help from the institution. On the other hand, Al was critically present to his own response-ability, feeling that there was something he should be doing to alleviate the plight of these students. Not to resist the practice was somehow a betrayal of the principal's own authenticity as an educator and citizen-administrator. Note that initially that critical presence to self was not to the self as an educational leader whose responsibility was to be proactive as well as reactive in that situation.

Examination of the qualities of critical presence offers, perhaps, the clearest evidence of the dialogical nature of presence. The self, in responding to the presence of the other, becomes aware of some blockage to or distortion of authentic communication. This awareness may lead to an attempt to clarify what is going on and what is at stake in the situation. That clarification, in turn, may call forth a more genuinely authentic presence on the part of one or both of the parties. In this way, the virtue of presence mediates the dialogue between authenticity and responsibility. Awareness of something in their mutual presence that distorts their sense of themselves as authentic human beings or as authentic educators leads to a sense of responsibility to clear up the distortion so as to release the possibility of authentic communication.

Critical presence calls on us to name the problem that stands between us and the other. Naming of the problem, however, should not be one-sided. Both parties have to be present to the other, listen to each other, and then see what the situation asks of both. In some cases, what the situation asks of us may be unacceptable because it violates who we are or violates other responsibilities that outweigh the demands of the other. In a situation where a principal has repeatedly encountered refusal to engage in the communal work of improving student learning, critical presence may lead to a request that the teacher leave the school.

Critical presence should not be a haphazard occurrence. It should be an enduring predisposition that acknowledges ahead of time the reality of messes that humans make—interpersonal, institutional, and policy messes. Critical presence is not based on cynicism but rather on compassion and hope for the human condition. It is based on compassion for a humanity that aspires to heroic ideals yet whose fragility and vulnerability lead to overestimating possibilities or to shrinking back in fear of the risks involved. It is based on hope for a humanity that has demonstrated time and again a resilience that transforms oppressive situations into opportunities for heroic and courageous transcendence of the human spirit.

Critical presence allows no alibi for inauthenticity. It calls on us to respond to the other, to listen carefully to what it tells us about itself, and to respond to what it asks of us. Inauthentic presence "embodies a neglectful indifference to that which calls for a response" (Anton, 2001, p. 155). Critical presence has to be continual, not haphazard or convenient. Just as "we cannot be authentic every once in a while" (Anton, 2001), we have to be continually critically present to ourselves and our propensity to fall back into self-seeking behavior, as well as critically present to those persons, policies, or institutional practices that impede our proactive leadership responsibilities.

We can also recognize that critical presence is often the precursor to affirming presence. A critic is expected to point out the praiseworthy aspects of a performance as well as its shortcomings. Critical presence can also have a cleansing effect on our affirming presence, being critically on the lookout for self-serving affirmation that so easily turns into manipulation.

Enabling Presence

This third form of ethical presence flows from the prior forms of ethical presence—affirming presence and critical presence—because through them one acts to respond to the possibilities and the predicaments of the other, to the enabling or limiting aspects of situations and arrangements. An enabling presence starts with this premise: I can't do it alone; you can't do it alone; only *we* can do it. An enabling presence signifies that one brings oneself fully into the situation with the other person. Again, the institutional setting of the school, with all its limitations as well as its potential, its constraints as well as its capacities, contextualizes every situation. Enabling leaders explore dialogically how to enable a person to be more successful with students, how to develop a pedagogy that will serve a teacher's classroom effectiveness as well as bring a greater sense of personal fulfillment and satisfaction in the work.

Sometimes that enabling presence is predominantly a listening presence when a teacher or parent needs to explain a problem or to propose an idea that could be adopted by the school. In that case, an enabling presence communicates a respect for the other, as well as a confidence that the other may already have the answer they are seeking but need to explore its dimensions more explicitly. An enabling presence also has to trust the good judgment of the other in the process of letting them try out something that is quite new to the school. The enabling leader is also a responsible leader who communicates a mutual taking of responsibility for the risks involved and therefore the need to surround new ideas with the appropriate safeguards and institutional supports.

In other circumstances, an enabling presence might be more proactive, encouraging teachers to look at various examples of research-grounded best practices that might be adapted to their own teaching and learning environments. Some administrators' enabling presence leads to a more institutionalized practice of teacher-run leadership advisory committees, through which teachers are supported in establishing project teams of teachers who will explore new technologies for instruction, new assessment techniques, or the development of in-house rubrics for looking at student work. Taking it further, some administrators' enabling presence will encourage groups of students to develop their own initiatives for peer tutoring, new aspects of student government, or student-led ways to resolve conflicts among the student body.

This kind of enabling presence is concerned with capacity building—that is, building whatever capacities are needed to improve learning. With the national emphasis on school improvement, capacity building appears at the top of administrators' agenda (Adams and Kirst, 1999). What I am suggesting here is that capacity building is not simply a matter of policy implementation. It is also a matter of deep conviction about the ways in which human beings ought to be present to one another and bringing that conviction into the institutional setting of the school—whether or not the state policymakers think it is a good idea.

The leader's enabling presence takes account of the institutional mission and the institutional constraints and possibilities of schools. An enabling presence, however, also brings an affirming presence, a spirit of openness to others, a welcoming of people as they are: a mix of talents and interests, hopes and fears, strengths and fragilities. What is possible for the school, for teachers, and for students will be constrained by institutional policies and resources, to be sure, but those constraints can be transformed into possibilities and those possibilities enlarged by the creativity and talent of teachers and students who feel affirmed.

The leader's enabling presence will have to attend to building specific capacities among the teachers, given the agenda of school reform. Those capacities include greater diagnostic sensitivity to how children learn and do not learn; greater attentiveness to so-called low-achieving students in order to unlock their learning potential and to provide the institutional supports they need in order to improve; a more careful calibration of school rubrics for assessment and state rubrics for assessment; a more diversified approach to teaching higher-order thinking and creativity; and a deeper familiarity with diverse cultures in order to bring insights from those cultures into the classroom to enrich the learning of all.

The leader's enabling presence should also encourage each teacher to use his or her creativity to enliven learning in his or her classroom. It is possible to implement the so-called school improvement capacity-building lists by using the same old deadening, soporific classroom pedagogies. To be sure, teachers are not in the entertainment business. But classrooms definitely need an enormous infusion of imagination, humor, and adventure to invigorate and optimize the learning process. Rationality is a good thing, but humans are not simply logic machines. They need to perceive the underlying drama in life and sense the beauty and the pathos, the mystery and the complexity of the world in order to be attracted to studying the world. Leaders who bring an enabling presence into the classroom will discuss with teachers how to make classroom learning come alive. They won't be satisfied with one new teaching strategy. They will keep coming back until classrooms bubble with excitement and enthusiasm.

Leaders with an enabling presence will develop what is known as a spirit of efficacy among the teachers and students (Ashton and

Webb, 1986). That spirit signifies that teachers, both individually and collectively, grow to believe that there is no student that they cannot reach, that there is no pedagogical problem that they cannot find reasonable solutions to when they put their mind and imagination to work. A spirit of efficacy is not a Pollyannaish claim of omnipotence; rather, it is a pragmatic understanding that every situation can be improved, not to perfection, of course, but increasingly over time. Similarly, the enabling presence of administrators and teachers can lead students to develop an attitude of efficacy, of "I can do this" or "we can do this." This is not to deny the reality of temporary failure. But the efficacious attitude toward learning expects to learn from failure and to make improvements the next time around.

By contrast, the administrator who is half present to teachers and students comes to accept average performance as good enough, to be satisfied that the school is performing well if the teachers are at the front of the room and the students are in their seats, there are no fights in the cafeteria, and the football team wins some of their games. The half-present administrator fails to see how much time is being wasted every day: students' time wasted by boring classes, teachers' time wasted by filling out forms and attending meetings at which teaching and learning are trivialized into bits and pieces. The half-present administrator fails to see the enormous potential that resides in every teacher and every student, a potential that is anesthetized by school routines that ensure a modicum of control and a minimum of commitment to the work of learning. The enabling administrator brings an enormous reservoir of hope and expectation to encounters with teachers and students, keeps asking questions like "Is that all?" "Is that all you expect of the students?" "Is that all you expect from going to school?" "Is that all we expect of ourselves?"

Elsewhere (Starratt, 2003), I have written about various levels of empowerment: bureaucratic, professional, moral, and existential. At a minimal level of bureaucratic empowerment, the leader's enabling presence may empower teachers to participate more democratically in addressing organizational issues at the school. The leader's enabling presence can also empower teachers to own their professional development, embracing the school's efforts in capacity building and bringing to that effort the force of their own personal talents and creativity. Beyond that, the leader's enabling presence can empower teachers to take responsibility for their institutional responsibilities to their students. At that point, as Bauman (1995) suggests, morality becomes consciously engaged as we take responsibility for our intuited human sense of responsibility *to be for the other*.

Finally, the leader's enabling presence, after a trial period in which trust is mutually tested and mutually embraced, invites the other to existential empowerment. Here is where affirming presence joins enabling presence. That level of being present is not offered easily, nor is it offered unconditionally; rather, it is offered within the constraints and possibilities of the institution. The leader says by this presence that "It's good to be who you are; let your work express who you are and who you are becoming." Existential empowerment means that one is free to bring oneself fully into the work of teaching, to cocreate the sacred moments of learning with others and in those moments to *find* oneself.

Table 4.1 summarizes the ethics of presence presented in this chapter. As we have seen, the three ways of being present tend to complement one another.

Responsibility, Authenticity, and Presence

Now that we have examined these virtues separately, let us examine how they work together. Humans experience themselves as "thrown into life" (Heidegger, 1962). "We must decide and take responsibility for the commitments and projects we give ourselves. To live in this way is to be authentic, to be true to ourselves. However, taking responsibility for ourselves can be a burden; it can be

Table 4.1. The Ethics of Presence for Educational Leaders

- Presence means a full awareness of self and other. It suggests full attention to the other. It implies being close, being toward, being for.

- Presence is intrinsically and necessarily dialogical: a dialogue between the self as subject and the self as an object of critique or affirmation; a dialogue between the self as subject and the other as object; an intersubjective dialogue between the self and the other, who are mutually and authentically communicating.

- Presence has at least three primary characteristics, which sometimes function alone and frequently function together.

  - Affirming presence: the self affirms the other as a distinct, authentic being in its own right and affirms the ontological right of the other to be what or who it is.

  - Critical presence: the self is present both to itself as a source of blockage or distortion of authentic communication with the other and to what in the other blocks or distorts authentic communication. In both cases, critical presence helps to name the problem dialogically and remove it from blocking or distorting the possibility of authentic communication.

  - Enabling presence: the self invites the other to exercise the other's autonomy and actual or potential talents in carrying out their common work. Enabling presence invites the other's involvement at various levels of increased participation in the work of the institution: the bureaucratic, professional, moral, and existential levels.

- The three expressions of presence constitute an ethics of presence that mediates the relationship between the leader's ethics of authenticity and ethics of responsibility.

isolating and, at times, awesome" (Bonnet and Cuypers, 2003, p. 328). As we make these choices, we must be aware that there are no correct answers. Ultimately, whatever their source, we are the ones who must choose the values and norms that will bind us. We make them binding. Thus, the pragmatic ground of our ethics is that we choose to be bound by their norms. We choose them; only through the mediation of our freedom do they choose us.

Thus, to be authentic, I have to take responsibility for the self I choose to be. To be responsible, I have to choose to be authentic. But to be authentic and responsible, I have to be present to my authentic self and be present to the circumstances and situations so that I can connect my authentic self to the roles I have chosen to play. Presence is the switch that, when it's on, connects my authenticity to my situational responsibilities and connects those responsibilities to my responsibility to be myself in those circumstances.

Being thus connected, I am in touch with my fundamental freedom—my choice to be authentic and bear responsibility (being able to respond to others and to myself as to why I am doing this rather than that) or to shrink back, modify, temporize by choosing an activity that is political, self-serving, defensive, aggressive, manipulative (and thus refuse to be responsible). The choice to be authentic in any given situation may involve a choice to be less candid or transparent, to compromise in order to get half the desired result. But in making such a choice, if one is to be authentic, one must recognize that it is only one of a series of choices stretching into the future that are organically connected to a long-range strategy of authentically exercising one's life choices.

Holding this idea of choices that move by increments toward a larger realization of one's authentic life is not only normal but probably the most deeply moral choice and series of choices. Authenticity has to be dialogical, both asserting self and receiving the other. In receiving the other—a spouse, a tax collector, a daily schedule, a science curriculum, a state policy of high-stakes testing—one has to accept the other's legitimate claims and the responsibilities they seek to impose on us. Being authentic, then, is not simply the unconditional exercise of my freedom to express myself and impose myself on the universe. Rather, authenticity is realized in dialogue. The conditions of dialogue present both possibilities and limitations for my self-expression (Taylor, 1991; Bonnet and Cuypers, 2003). But it is in the dialogue that authenticity becomes moral, for it involves the negotiation of who I am in relationship to the full reality of what the other is. That negotiation, in order to be moral, must not violate the intrinsic integrity of the other, although the negotiation may involve my influence over the other in such a way that the integrity of the other is more fully realized. This ongoing flow of dialogical negotiation with the other is the essence of the moral life. In that negotiation, one can discern the virtuous activity of dialogical authenticity, dialogical presence, and dialogical responsibility: the foundations of a moral life.

How does this ethic apply to the activity of moral educational leadership? First, it demonstrates that those educators who would lead are called to an exemplary exercise of these virtues. What distinguishes exceptional educational leaders from their colleagues is the intensity and depth with which they exercise these virtues in their work. Their role as educators necessarily involves their humanity as well as their role as citizens. The work of education is a deeply human work, and it is intrinsically a work of citizenship as well. The authentic and responsible educator is one whose own authenticity is channeled and poured out in authentic relationships with learners, in authentic relationship to the activity of learning itself, and in authentic relationship to the human, academic, and civic curriculum that constitutes the joint work with student-learners. Because those relationships are dialogical, they impose responsibility not only to one's own authenticity but to the student-learner, to the activity of learning, and to the threefold curriculum that defines the common work of students and educators. What enables this dialogue of authentic relationships and intersecting responsibilities is the virtuous activity of presence, the mutual presence of educator and student-learner, their mutual presence to the unfolding learning process, and their mutual presence to the threefold curriculum.

The dynamic influence that each virtue exercises on the other two generates the moral reflection and action of an educational leader. The leader's responsibilities as a human being, as an educator, as a citizen, and as an administrator challenge her or him to be authentic in all of those roles (see Figure 4.1). To enter into the mutual dialogue that authenticity requires, the leader has to be present to the authenticity of the other. That implies a presence that is affirming, critical, and enabling, as well as a presence that invites authentic communication in return.

The other is not always a person or a group of persons; it is sometimes the work activity itself, which has its own integrity. The activity of learning has its own authentic character; it is an inquiry into

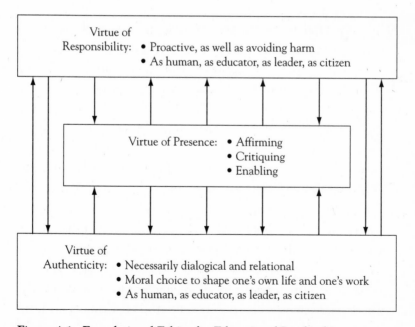

Figure 4.1. Foundational Ethics for Educational Leadership

meaning, significance, value, connection with other learnings, connection with actual or potential lived experience, and connection to ways humans interact with and participate in the world. So, too, the other can be the academic curriculum, which has its own integrity as a body of knowledge based on the scholarly methodology that produced it. Teachers' authenticity as teachers requires them to respect and dialogue with the authenticity of each discipline. Thus, their authenticity as teachers places a proactive responsibility on them to stay abreast of developments in the disciplines they are teaching. The authenticity of the educational leader in dialogue with teachers imposes the proactive responsibility to encourage and enable the teachers to stay current in their fields. The critical presence of the leader to the curriculum may call attention to its superficiality, its bias, or its avoidance of important social issues. This critical presence, in turn, leads the leader to exercise proactive responsibility to discuss and correct these curriculum deficiencies with the teaching staff.

The educational leader has to be present to the school's attention to the human development of students, to both the obstacles and the possibilities embedded in the way the school is organized. The leader's presence facilitates organizational attention to the learning situation of students and also to the development of civic responsibilities within students. The organizational attention will either be authentic or inauthentic. The organizational resources devoted to these areas of student development will be adequate, effective, and documentable, or they will be inadequate, ineffective, and ephemeral—that is, inauthentic, fake, unreal, a weak imitation of the real thing. By being present to the organization and its activity as an obstacle to or an enabler of the core work of the school, the authentic leader recognizes her or his proactive responsibility to change the way the organization of the school works. In the case of Al Auther, his authenticity as an educator led him to a vague sense of his responsibility to respond to the opportunity-to-learn issue for some of his students. However, we might question whether he was present to the apparent widespread inauthenticity of the teaching and learning work of the school and to the contribution that organizational arrangements made to this inauthenticity.

Beyond the dynamic exercise of the virtues of responsibility, authenticity, and presence in the reflection and action of the educational leader, we can see how the moral work of the leader should involve the development of these virtues throughout the school community. The leader should promote these virtues among teachers and students. The leader should appeal to the teachers to be true to what they profess, to engage the students in authentic relationships, and to design their pedagogy to catalyze authentic learning. Furthermore, the leader should challenge the students, in collaboration with the rest of the community, to take more responsibility for coproducing the school as a human place for authentic learning and for practicing civility and civic responsibilities.

Through the work of the teachers, students need to be encouraged to be more fully present to one another, affirming both their cultural differences and the common humanity they enjoy. Teachers and students also need to find ways to be more fully present to the learning activities in the curriculum. Being responsible to the authenticity of learning means also being present to the integrity of what is being studied, whether that is a poem, the life of a cell, the Industrial Revolution, the grammatical structure of a sentence, or applications of the algebraic slope-y-intercept formula. Through authentic learning, students let the curriculum speak back to them about the challenges and possibilities of their world and more fully engage their minds, hearts, and imaginations as they coproduce the knowledge they will need to participate in that world.

The virtues of responsibility, authenticity, and presence are basic to the reflection and action of moral educational leaders. There is a logic to the dynamic relationship among the virtues. Responsibility returns to authenticity for its subjective grounding and moral weight;

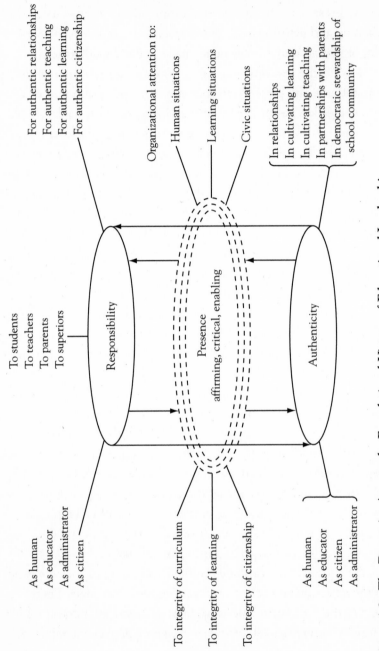

Figure 4.2. The Dynamics Among the Foundational Virtues of Educational Leadership

through affirming and critical presence, authenticity establishes the necessary dialogue with the other's authenticity or inauthenticity; authenticity enacts responsibility in expressing a positive or negative moral response. Presence is the medium between authenticity and responsibility. Authenticity needs both presence and responsibility; responsibility expresses both presence and authenticity. The three virtues interpenetrate and complement each other. As Figure 4.2 shows, the exercise of these three virtues provides a foundation for an ethics of moral educational leadership. The dynamic interplay between these virtues must ground any more formally explicit ethics of educational leadership, whether it is an ethics of justice, an ethics of care, or a synthesis of several ethical perspectives (Furman, 2003; Maxcy, 2002; Noddings, 1992; Shapiro and Stefkovich, 2001; Starratt, 1991; Strike, Haller, and Soltis, 1998).

Our ethical analysis has highlighted three foundational virtues for educational leadership: the virtue of taking responsibility, the virtue of being authentic, and the virtue of being fully present. Further, we see those virtues being applied to three dimensions within the situation of schooling: the human dimension, the academic dimension, and the civic dimension. Thus, an ethical educational leader has to be responsible to and for all three dimensions, has to be present to all three dimensions, and has to be authentic within all three dimensions.

In the next chapter, we will return to the last act of our morality play. We will observe Al Auther as he uses his clearer moral understanding to map out a strategic plan for his leadership.

5

Giving Birth to Virtue

A l Auther has had an unsettling two weeks since his last conversation with Margaret Wissen. He has been seeing himself
as well as Roosevelt Middle School in a new light, and it has not
been pleasant. He has entered into a deeper presence to himself on
the job. He has been much more aware of how perpetually distracted he is by continual interruptions in his daily schedule,
whether it is a phone call from a disgruntled parent, an e-mail from
the superintendent requesting yet another report for the state
department of education, a problem student sent to the office for
the second time that week, a call from the cafeteria to come to the
aid of a teacher having difficulty breaking up a shouting match
among two groups of students, a teacher requesting curriculum
resources for which there is no more money left in the budget, or a
call from the fire department notifying him that there would be
a fire drill some time during the next two weeks. Almost all of his
energies are being absorbed in reacting to situations. He is expected
to be the fix-it-man: fix this child; fix this teacher; fix this child's
class schedule; fix the low scores on the state tests. He sees, on reflection, that he enjoys playing that role; it gives him a sense that
he is involved in the lives of people, helping them to cope, keeping
the school from descending into chaos. That last phrase, "descending into chaos," keeps coming back to him. Something inside him is

nudging him to look at that phrase again. Why is the school so consistently on the verge of chaos?

When he plays back the memory reels of his daily experiences, he sees students sitting in classrooms, some sullen, some daydreaming, some fooling around, some passing notes back and forth to a friend, some trying to follow the teacher's explanation on the blackboard. He sees teachers working in isolation, some trying creative adaptations of the textbook material, most simply following the textbook page by page and using the exercises at the end of each chapter. He plays the reel of his visits to the teachers' room. Some teachers are off in corners correcting homework; others are absorbed in reading the newspaper. A cluster of teachers are complaining about this week's students from hell, and a few teachers are talking about the car they would buy if they had the money.

Al plays back reels of walking through corridors filled with students during class breaks. Some gather by the stairwell with their friends to plan their after-school activities. Others walk in a seeming stupor to their locker to toss in one set of books and pick out another set for the next class. Still others laugh about something stupid another student said in the previous class.

As Al has walked around the school for the past two weeks with a sense of "almost chaos," it has gradually became apparent that "almost chaos" suggests that everyone in the school seems to be going their own way. Although there is a daily class schedule, everyone seems to have a different idea about how they are to spend their class time. Despite the variety of activities in the school, there is no sense that the community is working with a united purpose. There are more than nine hundred individual agendas being pursued under one roof.

Among the majority of students, the agenda seems to be to survive the daily grind of classes so they can be with their friends. There is little sense among this group of students that schoolwork has any meaning that is really connected to their lives. The really important work for these students is to figure out how to be accepted, how to fit in with the right group, and how to cope with family issues—whether they involve living in a crowded apartment with three younger siblings and a single mother on welfare or surviving the relentless criticism of overly demanding parents. For others, the really important work is making the team; for still others, it's how to save enough money to buy a computer like the one the kid down the street has. Coming to school is something that adults require them to do. They are familiar with the party line: all this schoolwork will pay off when they apply to college or apply for a job. But there is no fun in schoolwork. Fun takes place after school. "Let's face it, Al," the principal concludes, "the happiest day of the year for most of these kids is the first day of summer holidays."

As Al Auther looks more closely, he realizes that the teachers aren't having much fun, either. There is little sense of fascination with the knowledge they are bringing to the students. It is material to be covered. Rarely does he find a teacher opening class with a puzzle or a game. Seldom does he hear teachers ask their students, "What would you do in this situation?" or "How would you feel in this predicament?" or "How would you use this knowledge if you were in charge of a community agency that was supposed to deal with this issue?" or "How would you write a song about that?" Most of the time, teachers trudge through the curriculum material, one unit after another, with the occasional warning that "this material could be on the state test, so you'd better pay attention and learn this." In his visits to classrooms, the most imaginative teachers tend to be the special education teachers.

By and large, however, the school resembles a collection of factory workers who resignedly march off to work every day with their lunch pails, to put in a day's work. The satisfying elements of students' and teachers' lives exist outside of the school and its predictable everyday routines. They do the work without much reflection, as though some intangible force requires them to plod on.

There is nothing transformative about the work, little sense of any dramatic significance, and hardly any hope that this work could—even in a small way—alter history, let alone lead to a deeply satisfying personal life.

As Al thinks about it, he sees that the "close to chaos" condition of the school seems to reflect two general phenomena. One is that the common work of learning and the teaching that is supposed to stimulate it is seen by the students as boring, abstracted from the reality of their lives, evaluated by seemingly arbitrary and punitive procedures, and never really legitimated by those in charge. The punishments for noncooperation are severe enough—parental nagging and removal of home-based privileges; censure and humiliation by school personnel in the assessment labels that they pin on each student; remedial classes after school, on Saturdays, and during the summer; disqualification from playing on school teams—to induce the minimal compliance necessary to pass (or even to get an A). Students who take their work seriously and ask the kinds of questions that show deep understanding are exceptions, not the rule. Getting an A in a course is not necessarily an indication of that level of understanding, either.

The teachers, worn down by years of student resistance and minimal compliance, accept a modified definition of their work: keeping control, presenting the material—sometimes with enthusiasm and sensitivity—with the expectation that, due to the inattention of the students and the multiple distractions in their lives, it will require several attempts to get them sufficiently on task to pass the weekly quiz. Passing the weekly quiz, however, is simply an indication, in many cases, of partial and fleeting engagement with the curriculum.

It is becoming clearer to Al that the second source of the "almost chaos" at Roosevelt Middle School is a result of the first general condition of anomie about the common work of the school. It leads both students and teachers to seek satisfaction in their daily lives in personal relationships, in family events, in hobbies, team sports, and recreational activities, not in school activities. Since there is little to bond people together in communal, purposeful activity, everyone's agenda is personal. Al recognizes that even he has often felt the tug to leave work earlier, to get home to play with his three-year-old son before the evening meal.

That realization gives him further pause. People have lives outside of school. They have legitimate concerns to take care of, important relationships to sustain, involvements in neighborhood and community groups and organizations. He can't judge them as lacking in professional or academic commitment because they value the important elements in their lives outside of school. The problem isn't the out-of-school commitments; the problem is that the work inside the school lacks those qualities of enthusiasm and satisfaction for staff and students both personally and collectively.

Returning his focus to the school, Al sees more clearly that everyone seems to be pursuing a personal agenda. He realizes that easily half of the things he is required to fix have their origins in these individual agendas of students and teachers. Students get into trouble for skipping classes to sneak off with their friends, for hanging out with their friends at night instead of doing their homework, for watching their favorite TV show instead of studying for the weekly quiz. Teachers squabble over class schedules, parking spaces, union policies, and after-school duties. Because students and teachers do not having a major focus such as collaborating on a compelling common agenda, minor irritations escalate into significant problems for Al to fix.

With an uncomfortable shock, Al realizes that he already knew this about student and teacher attitudes. Now he understood that he had been, at best, half present to these realities. He realizes that he has been part of the problem, not because he has been doing something wrong, but because he has been blind to the challenge of what was staring him in the face. He has been flailing about, taking responsibility to fix symptoms of a much larger problem. Even his concern about the special needs and second-language learners having an adequate opportunity to learn ignores the larger problem of widespread disengagement from the common work of the school. These students are at risk because of the high-stakes tests but are more at risk because the whole school is working well below its capacity. Now that he is more fully present to the students' and teachers' minimal engagement with the core work of the school, that reality speaks back to him: "So what are you going to do about it, big boy?"

With this clearer sense of what he is dealing with, Al realizes that he needs some private time to face himself and decide what is the authentic response for him. When he shares his thoughts with his wife, she cautions him not to take the whole weight of the situation onto his shoulders alone. Everyone has made their choices in life. Granted that institutional conditions have limited those choices, everyone has to take some responsibility for living and behaving the way they have. Al sees the wisdom of her caution. He recognizes his tendency to take the whole load of a situation on himself. His wife suggests that he call her cousin who has a cabin on a nearby lake, where he might get away for a day or two. A phone call secures the cabin for later in the week. Al arranges to take two personal days off from the office, and two days later sets out for the cabin for his reflective time.

Readers' Reflection Time

Assume that you have come to the same conclusions about the "close to chaos" condition of Roosevelt Middle School. Imagine yourself taking a two-day retreat at a lakeside cabin to figure out what your leadership response to the situation should be. Notice that I said "should be" rather than "might be." "Should" implies a moral responsibility to yourself and to the stakeholders in the school. But notice also that there are few explicit rules to tell you what you should do. It is up to you to exercise your personal, professional, and civic discretion in facing a very complex situation.

This exercise involves identifying your substantive responsibilities as well as the process for carrying out those responsibilities.

Assuming that you are grounded in the foundational virtues of responsibility, authenticity, and presence, what kinds of questions do you need to answer for *yourself*? What kinds of questions do you need to pose to the students, their teachers, and their parents? After these reflections, try to lay out a strategy for your moral leadership of Roosevelt Middle School over the next two to three years. When you have worked through this exercise, return to Al Auther as he begins his retreat.

Al Auther's Retreat

Al arrives at the cabin a little before 9:00 A.M. By the time he has stored his provisions, walked down to the lake's edge to get a sense of the place while the coffee brews, and set up his work space at the kitchen table, it is close to 10:00. He pours his first cup of coffee and takes up his notepad. As he constructs a timetable for himself, working backward from his planned departure at 4:00 P.M. the next day, he realizes that he won't have enough time to go into issues very thoroughly, but he can try to identify the most important issues and how he might respond to them.

The first issue he writes down is "ME." Al knows that he needs to look at himself. The business of authenticity that was raised in his conversation with Margaret Wissen needs a close look now. On one hand, Al does not want to be bullied by his conscience into embracing a hopelessly idealistic leadership posture, one that holds little prospect of success but that would leave him the consolation of being able to say to his grandchildren, "I was true to my values. I refused to compromise or be compromised." Nevertheless, his authenticity as a human being, as an educator, as a citizen-administrator and as an educational leader is at stake. "How can I be real and be realistic at the same time?" he asks. He immediately knows the answer. The only way to be real is to be realistic. Being realistic, however, does not mean accepting the status quo. Being realistic means looking at institutional and cultural constraints as challenges that will require a large and coordinated effort in order to transform them from constraints into enablers.

Al underscores those words in his notebook: <u>be real by being be realistic—turn institutional constraints into enablers</u>. He recognizes these words as a potential leadership motto for himself. His leadership—his moral leadership—has to involve him in bringing the students, the teachers, and the school to an awareness of, a presence to the dysfunctionality of their present minimal engagement of the work of the school—the work that legitimates their membership in that school.

Al drew back. "I can't do this as some kind of enlightened wisdom figure sitting in judgment over their minimizing the work of the public institution of schooling. I've been part of that dysfunctional community for years, as a teacher and now as a principal. This is not their problem; it is *our* problem. But how do I say that without some of them feeling accused? Somehow I have to stress the positive—the possibilities we are called to—instead of criticizing the mediocre realization of those possibilities. I somehow have to bring them to the same realization that I came to about responsibility—that it should be a proactive concern for realizing the good—rather than try to explain or justify our part in a dysfunctional system.

"But I have to come back to me. Can I do this? Am I up to the complexity and commitment of this kind of leadership? Do I want to risk the clear possibility of rejection, perhaps the loss of my job if resisters turn this effort into a political fiasco?"

At this point, Al gets up to stretch. He decides to take a walk down by the lake and get some fresh air. He strolls along a path by the lake and comes to a stand of birch trees where there is a convenient rock for sitting by the water's edge. He resumes his sense of presence to himself—he finds himself using that term, which was suggested by Professor Wissen—and continues what has become a kind of interrogation. "Do I really want to do this?" he asks himself. Al feels something stir inside of him, and his insides start talking back to him. "Look, what you are pointing toward with fear and trembling is something I *want* to do. It's what my life has been moving toward. This is *real* work, not tinkering, not just getting through the day. Sure it's risky, but the risk is what calls you out of hiding. Besides, you'll find some people there who have been waiting for this invitation. You already know that you can't do it by yourself. So you start by seeking out potential allies. Share your ideas with them, but don't present those ideas as a definitive interpretation. Instead, put them out as an attempt to make sense of a complex situation. See how others respond. They might have additional interpretations that fill out your ideas, or they might find your interpretation overly pessimistic. The important thing is to create some common understandings and agreements about the reality of the situation and what should be done about it.

"And remember, if you're not sure you're up to the challenge, think of your teachers and students. You are asking them to take the same kind of risks, perhaps even greater ones. You're asking them to let go of the daily satisfactions of their personal agendas and minimal commitment to the school agenda in order to risk the uncertainties of working together at something really different, something perhaps quite difficult. You are asking them to invest in a level of learning that requires putting their own authenticity on the line. You'll have to go there gently, but you cannot *not* go there."

Al hears himself talking back with conviction, almost a passion. That voice seems very much like the real Al, the Al he wants to be. He finds himself more at peace as he walks back to the cabin to fix himself a light lunch. It seems that his real self has made the decision for him. The challenges are still there, but they don't frighten him as much as they did before. He is accepting responsibility for leadership. This is what he should be doing.

Al's Lists

After lunch Al makes a list of the members of his teaching staff and puts plus signs after as many of them as he can, noting his hunch about their willingness to join a major restructuring of the school and the specific talents they can bring to the task. He has identified the eight regular classroom teachers and three special education teachers who exhibit the most talent and commitment among the thirty-seven members of the teaching staff. He can start with some or all of this group to open the conversation about turning the school around. He thinks the other three special education teachers and roughly another twelve of the general classroom teachers will join the effort, once the conversations have developed enough clarity to provide a clear sense of what the initial steps might be. Of the other teachers, some are too new to the school to be able to tell, some are close to retirement and might continue to coast for their final few years, and some have the talent but have turned to blaming everyone else for the sorry state of the school.

"Overall," Al thinks, "I've got a pretty good critical mass on the staff who could make this thing happen; they just need to be invited in the right way. They have to see the transformation of the school as a real possibility, as something that will happen through very pragmatic steps, each of which is reasonably within their grasp. But there is the first step of getting them to look at themselves as teachers, to get back in touch with their ideals and their lost enthusiasm." That appeal will call on Al's own deepest reserves of ideals and convictions as an educator and as a human being. He will have to reach a level of conversation with them that he has never dared, never even thought about. He will have to talk with them about—it sounds so platitudinous as he tries to write it down—the meaning of their lives, not just their individual lives but their lives together, and what they can make happen with the youngsters if they tap into the deepest reserves of their humanity as energy sources for their teaching. Somehow they have to reach that level of conversation, and from there build the trust in each other that they are in this thing together. They need to share dreams of what the school could become if learning were really exciting, interesting, connected to the lives of the students. Dreaming of what can be will open up the space for them to imagine how to make it happen. Al will have to spend a lot of time composing his opening appeal to the teachers. It will have to come from his heart. It will also have to point to something clear, realistic, practical, and . . . *fulfilling* for them.

Al also knows that together, he and the teachers will have to compose an appeal to the students, an appeal that speaks from their hearts to the hearts of the students. It, too, will have to point to something that is clear, realistic, connected to practical aspects of their lives, and also fulfilling. What will they offer the students? That has to be worked out. And so Al turns to his next list, a brainstorming of ideas about the present and the possible curriculum of the school.

Al knows that whatever curriculum they devise will have to meet district expectations and state standards and guidelines. Al believes, however, that there are ways to infuse that curriculum with personal meaning, excitement, and creative inquiry and expression for students as individuals and for students as members of learning teams. Al and the teachers have to find a way to create a general enthusiasm for learning, a sense that the world that the students engage in the curriculum is indeed their world, a world that needs them, a world that welcomes their participation, a world filled with challenges as well as with wonders and fascinating intricacies, a world where they can both define themselves and find themselves.

If Al and the teachers can engage the general student body in learning that is important and personally absorbing for them and that implicates them both personally and communally in responding to and taking responsibility for the world, then that sense of learning will likely infect the second-language learners and special needs students. Moreover, if average and bright students become excited about their schoolwork, their deeper involvement in the learning process might lead to some promising initiatives in peer tutoring and in big brother or big sister relationships between the older students and the younger students, especially those entering the school in the fifth grade.

Al jots down about twenty ideas under the heading "Making Learning Come Alive." He knows that these ideas are simply starters for much longer conversations with teachers. While he is working on the list, he feels a surge of energy. When he checks out the feeling, he realizes that he is enjoying brainstorming these possibilities. This is authentic educational work.

Al begins a new list under the heading "In-House Obstacles to Learning." He writes down some possible culprits: the daily schedule of forty-six-minute periods; the isolation of academic disciplines from one another, which smothers any flexibility to apply two or three curriculum areas to a substantial project; the relentless need to cover the syllabus; the isolated classroom, which prevents teachers from working together; a weekly schedule in which every day looks the same. Al stops writing to see what he has. The list surprises him. He had been only half present to those obstacles; they had simply defined the way his school worked. They had the solid appearance of reality, yet they were as socially constructed as the reality of this year's style in neckties. Yet even his half-presence to the obstacles had somehow fed into a reservoir of dissatisfaction at the back of his mind that had surfaced during this effort to look at new possibilities for learning.

Al also saw more clearly now that if these in-house obstacles to learning posed problems for bright and average students, they probably posed even more serious problems for underachieving students. He remembered his reading about "mastery learning" during his teacher-training years; research that shows that a large majority of students are capable of earning an A grade if they are given enough time and a variety of pedagogical approaches are used. In capital letters on his list of obstacles to learning, Al writes "TIME."

Al gets up to stretch and brews another pot of coffee. He steps out onto the cabin porch and notices how the afternoon sun makes everything a different color. He decides to work outside in the warm afternoon air and pulls a rocking chair onto the porch. Sipping a cup of fresh coffee, he starts a new list, "Diversity Issues." Under that heading he creates three subheadings: "Parents," "Students," and "Curriculum." Under "Parents," he jots: "Parents of different language communities and cultures need to have their own voice. . . . Create multiple sub-committees within the PTA. . . . They elect one or two representatives to the PTA board. . . . Increase PTA communications with school council. . . . Set up welcoming arrangements for parents of newly arrived second-language students." That list can be made longer, but Al wants to get to the students.

Under the "Students" heading, Al writes: "Need for student clubs that represent various language and cultural communities. . . . Need for principal to listen to members of those clubs in some kind of advisory capacity. . . . Those clubs to be in touch with their parent groups. . . . Have those clubs set up volunteer services in their communities as well as in the school, perhaps a tutoring service. . . . Have those clubs visit the feeder schools to talk to younger kids about coming to Roosevelt. . . . Have these clubs mediate some of the conflicts that arise among student groups, especially when the conflict implies a disparagement of one culture by another."

He then writes "Student Responsibilities" to start a new list. He writes: "Work on internalizing their sense of responsibility to themselves to learn how the world works and how they can participate in that world. . . . Have them take more responsibility for the public spaces in the school—for example, clean up after themselves in the cafeteria. . . . Take greater responsibility for counteracting bullying and scapegoating of fellow students. . . . Encourage volunteers for a variety of projects in the school—that coproduction thing!"

Knowing that there are more ideas to be included under the "Student Responsibilities" heading, Al nonetheless moves on to the "Curriculum" heading. There he writes: "Essential to have students apply much of their learning to family and neighborhood situations. . . . Apply learning to their own culture. . . . We need to have a wider variety of library books and literature that deals with the cultures that are represented in the school. . . . Make sure that sixth-grade social studies uses the unit on immigration, so that all the kids can relate it to their own family's experience. . . . Have a schoolwide assembly for sixth graders to present their immigration projects. . . . Check out the artwork displayed around the school; make it more representative of the art of the various cultures among the student body. . . . Any student art on permanent display? . . . Talk to the music teacher about broader exposure to and performance of music from the cultures represented in the student body. . . . Look into the possibility of performances at the school by various cultural groups in the community. . . . Have art and language teachers explore with students the commonalities across cultures, those things we share as human beings, as well as the distinctive expressions of their humanity in each culture."

Al's imagination is kicking into overdrive, so he pauses to look at what he has. He has the sense that he could fill a suitcase with these ideas. He hasn't gotten to the curriculum that is perhaps most ignored, the curriculum of community and civic responsibility. That would come next. But where is all this reflection taking him? Al leaves the porch and takes another stroll down to the lake.

As he looks to the farther shore across the lake, Al realized that the landscape of the positive possibilities for transforming the school is huge. He knows that he is just scratching the surface. He realizes that there will not be a problem finding examples of effective ways to make learning exciting. Any number of scholarly books and research reports can add to the ideas that the teaching staff will come up with. The issue is going to come down to choosing the most appealing ideas and then translating those ideas into practical learning activities that, on one hand, have a legitimate relationship to the state standards and, on the other, truly engage the interest and enthusiasm of the students. There also has to be some way for students to showcase their learning, to apply it to real issues in the larger world, and through all of this, to come to understand the logic of the academic disciplines that they will need to succeed in the upper grades. All of this implies that after the initial effort of convincing the teachers to embrace the ideals of learning that will captivate the minds and imaginations of students, there will be the very disciplined work of putting the pieces together.

Al realizes that leading this work will take a commitment to stay with it for the long haul. He checks with his inner self: "Is this what you want?" The answer comes back as a resounding "Yes, with all my heart!" Al goes inside the cabin to call his wife before starting up the grill for his chicken dinner. He will finish the lists later tonight and clear the ground for tomorrow's work of drawing up specific strategies for the next several months. He knows he'll have to talk with the superintendent and her assistants. He has an idea that he should check out his plans with one of the veteran principals in the district who has a reputation for thinking outside of the box. He knows that he is putting both feet in the water and that soon he will be swimming over his head. He won't be alone, though. The image lights up his imagination: "Yes! That's what schools are supposed to do—teach kids how to swim from one shore to another, to use their minds and imaginations to swim in the waters of life rather than stand on the beach taking pictures of it, to take responsibility for getting to other shores that open up new possibilities, and to explore those possibilities together."

Back to the Reader

At this point, the curtain goes down on our morality play. The skeptics in the audience shake their heads, feeling sorry for Al and predicting his eventual disillusionment at the hands of the teachers union, the traditionalists on the school board, and the entrenched bureaucrats in the central office. The romantics in the audience

cheer wildly for Al as they feel him leading them toward a transformed tomorrow. The realists in the audience applaud Al for coming to terms with himself and for exploring exciting possibilities for
his teachers and students: "You know, he just might pull it off. He'll
need plenty of luck; need to convince key players at central office;
need to create political allies on the teaching faculty . . . but it could
happen . . . I'd almost want to be a part of this." As you leave this
imaginary theater, what lessons do you take with you about the
ethics of educational leadership?

The Critics' Commentary

As we reflect on Al Auther's performance, several aspects of his
moral leadership rise to the surface. First, Al had to go through some
initial soul searching to clarify his moral unease with the high-stakes
testing situation. He needed to identify what was morally problematic in the situation and what his responsibilities were. He then had
to go through a kind of double-loop learning (Argyris, 1977), in
which he came to see the high-stakes testing situation as a symptom of the much larger problem of the disengagement of both students and teachers from authentic learning. That realization did not
happen all at once. He had to go through several conversations with
a very patient, Socratically disciplined professor, who pushed his
thinking far enough back from a surface reaction to events for Al
to acquire a deeper understanding of the proactive sense of responsibility one should expect from a leader. The conversations with
Professor Wissen enabled Al to return to his work at the school with
a certain affective distance. He climbed up into the balcony above
the dance floor, so to speak, in order to observe himself and others
carrying on the daily dance of school life from a different perspective (Heifetz and Linsky, 2002). What he saw from the balcony was
a student body largely disengaged from authentic learning, going
through the motions, by and large, but minimally complying with
the learning agenda of the school. He saw teachers who were iso-

lated, burned out, fighting the tide of student apathy and resentment just enough to get through the week, for whom the teaching
and learning agenda of the school appeared close to drudgery. He
came up against what Hodgkinson (1991) points out as the leadership imperative to promote the primary value of the organization
(in this case, authentic teaching and learning) as opposed to the
personal values of individual members, or group values. Al realized
that some of those personal values were indeed legitimate. He also
realized that a frontal attack on the disengagement of the members
of the school community from the primary work of the school,
authentic teaching and learning, would more than likely lead to
further resistance and alienation. The blame game would simply
end up with everyone shifting the blame onto someone else.
Besides, he himself was partly to blame. Rather, Al saw that he
must appeal to the members' own sense of authenticity in order to
open them up to the satisfactions and possibilities of authentic
teaching and learning.

We see here an example of the dynamic between the virtue of
authenticity and the virtue of responsibility. Al attempts to be authentic in thinking about the kind of authentic relationships he
wants with the teachers and students. That leads him to understand
the demands of authentic learning and what kind of teaching that
learning requires. He then sees a connection between establishing
authentic relationships with teachers and students and appealing to
their authenticity as they consider the authentic work of the school.
The logical flow from that grasping of the appeal of authentic learning leads to taking responsibility to make that kind of authentic
learning take place. Since no individual in the school community,
including Al, knows how to make that happen, the whole school
community has to work together to explore what authentic learning means and how it might be teased into realization.

In order for all of this to happen, however, Al had to become
present to himself at a deeper level, be present to the affective tone
among the student body and the teaching staff, be present to the

organizational culture and structures that affected the quality of learning in the school. Initially, that presence was critical, critical of the lack of opportunities to learn for many of his students. Then Al achieved a more critical presence to the general disengagement of most of the students from academic learning, a more critical presence to the lackluster performance of many teachers in response to their students' indifference to the learning agenda, and a more critical presence to himself as distracted from his proactive responsibilities. He saw that he had to change his own level of being present to teachers and students and to the core work of the school, authentic learning. He had to risk his own vulnerability to criticism and rejection and be present to teachers and students as one of them, rather than as the authority who controlled things in the school. That meant trusting his own best instincts as a human being and as an educator and trusting the others' best instincts as human beings and as learners and teachers.

Al realized that although he had some idea of what authentic learning might look like, he did not know how to make it happen. Probably many teachers did not know how to make it happen. The students probably had the best ideas of what authentic learning meant for them and how it could be made real in class. So there was a need for teachers to be dialogically present to the students as both the teachers and the students worked their way to a learning that was authentic, about which both could say, "This is real. This really means something. This is connected to life." Al had to bring students and teachers from purely physical and technical engagement with learning activity to learning activity as moral activity, as activity that mattered deeply and was of immense value to them and to their world. Again, we sense the dynamic flow from presence to authenticity to responsibility, not necessarily in a lockstep sequence, but more as part of an interpenetrating field of moral energy that is truly transformative. At the end of the play, Al is beginning to realize that his leadership has to involve and reflect his own transformation from an ordinary, mediocre educator into an authentic and responsible educator. He has to cultivate the very virtues in his teachers and students that are morally transforming him.

The curtain came down too soon, for the proof of Al's good resolves and planning would be seen in action. Will Al continue to protest the unfair treatment of the special needs and second-language students? How will Al respond to the first sign of resistance to his efforts to get the students engaged in authentic learning from teachers or parents? Will Al continue to return to Professor Wissen, or will he form or join a support group of other principals from within and outside of the district? How will he negotiate with the teachers' union to obtain the necessary time to work with his teachers? How will he win support for his plans with the central office, so that they provide at least vocal support, if nothing else? As with all good drama, however, the audience leaves with the satisfaction of seeing only the present transformation of the protagonist, not with the ongoing saga played out in all its endless details.

For the audience, however, the saga does continue to play out in all its endless details. Having viewed the morality play and the accompanying commentary on the ethics behind the three foundational virtues, what does the audience bring back to their work? The final chapter of this book draws some implications for practitioners in the very real drama of leading schools.

6

Implications for Leaders of Schools

I t is time to get back to the real world of educational leadership. We have taken time to reflect on those virtues that should ground the work of educational leaders. It would be unrealistic to expect an automatic transformation of our work and of ourselves after reading this book. On the other hand, we can join with colleagues and agree to weekly or monthly conversations that will pursue further understanding of the ideas presented in this book and improve our efforts to realize them in our work.

Readers of this book will draw implications for their own work. For some practitioners, reading the book may highlight the need for an authenticity audit of themselves. For others, it may encourage them to address injustices more courageously with their school board and central office personnel. For some professors in graduate programs in educational administration, it may occasion the use of ethically charged cases in their courses. For some superintendents, it might suggest a series of leadership seminars for the principals in their district. For some principals, it might prompt the formation of a support group of other principals in order to share concerns about ethical issues at their schools.

Implications for the Continuing Education of Leaders

This book has been written from the belief that many practicing administrators want to do the right thing in their leadership endeavors, but many of them have not had an opportunity to learn the analytical perspectives (the ethics of moral leadership) that would enable them to embrace a moral dimension of leadership that they are in fact searching for. School districts should be much more proactive in providing continuing education opportunities for their administrators, not simply so they can master new budgetary or implementation processes, but so they can also deepen their understanding of the moral responsibilities that their leadership entails.

Central office leaders might pool their resources with two or three districts in the surrounding area and hold a series of seminars for the principals and other administrators in their systems. These seminars could include some of the following activities:

• In groups of three to five and with the help of a facilitator, administrative leaders can be asked to describe a morally challenging situation that they have had to face (omitting, when necessary and appropriate, any identifying information about the parties involved). These morally challenging situations can be analyzed from the perspective of responsibility—responsibility as a human being, as an educator, and as a citizen-administrator; responsibility to whom; and responsibility for what. The administrators would then be asked how their own and the other parties' authenticity was challenged in the situation. They could then be asked to perform a double-loop analysis of the situation. (Single-loop analysis takes a problem or situation at face value, offers a response, and leaves it at that. Double-loop analysis identifies the problem and then asks whether there are underlying reasons for it. Is the problem a symptom of a larger problem in the organization? Is the problem arising because a larger issue in the organization is being ignored? Double-loop analysis identifies the larger or underlying issue and then suggests a long-term strategy to deal with it as well as the immediate problem.) The small-group discussions could go on for a whole morning. As this process was repeated on three or four more occasions, the administrators would begin to clarify their proactive leadership responsibilities, as well as develop fresh strategies to handle similar challenging situations.

• Another exercise involves a group of administrators doing an audit of their daily activities, in order to identify how much time they are giving to their leadership responsibilities in contrast to how much time they spend reacting to minor crises and unexpected intrusions into their day's plans. As they become clearer on their leadership responsibilities, they can brainstorm strategies for gaining more time to focus on those responsibilities.

• Districtwide teams of administrators can develop a casebook of fictitious situations (but ones based on several real cases), which could be augmented every six months or so. The casebook could become a stimulus for administrators to explore how they can deal with these cases from a leadership perspective of proactive responsibility. Some of their time would be spent developing strategies for moral responses to the cases, but more time would be spent in double-loop learning, in exploring how to change the institutional conditions that may have caused the problem to arise in the first place. As district teams, they can exemplify proactive leadership within the district.

• School districts can partner with nearby university administrator preparation programs to develop activities for aspiring administrator candidates, such as those described in the next section. Perhaps practicing administrators and administrator candidates can be paired in joint programs.

Implications for University Programs

What are some implications for university programs focused on the preparation of educational leaders? When one examines university preparation programs in school leadership, on the surface, at least, one finds a preponderant focus on the professional components of leadership and a minor, usually parallel attention to ethical matters that is not integrated with the professional components. Preparation programs have to move beyond the simplistic notion that having students analyze cases involving complex ethical issues and challenges satisfies their preparation to exercise moral leadership in the field. Those exercises are indeed helpful in bringing attention to the need for ethical clarity when arbitrating moral conflicts in schools. However, the analysis usually stays with the negative responsibilities of educators—what they should be avoiding or preventing—rather than using these cases in a double-loop learning process to analyze the larger moral issues that schools and their leaders have often been blind to.

Leadership preparation programs have to more continually challenge candidates to probe the grounding of their ethical principles and moral values as human beings, as educators, and as citizens. Some professors might resist this requirement, protesting that such work is too close to a religious ministry or to psychological counseling. Such resistance ignores the critical state that schools find themselves in and reflects a dysfunctional separation of professionalism from moral responsibility. Those who lead schools need to have moral depth and a well-articulated platform for the moral work of learning in the school, as well as a clear sense of how to proactively engage teachers and students in an authentic process of learning.

Graduate programs in educational leadership should therefore consider including the following elements, whether within a series of courses or through separate seminars scattered throughout the program.

• An *authenticity audit*. This is an exercise in self-reflection, in which students respond to questions such as the following:

1. Underneath the roles I play, who is the real me?

2. What gives me a sense of my inner authenticity?

3. What are the things I'm most afraid of, and why?

4. What gives me strength to deal with difficult challenges?

5. What values do I hold that will guide me in my life and my work?

6. What are the significant experiences that have helped me so far in my personal life and in my career?

7. How do I contribute to or make a difference in the lives of others?

8. What kinds of characteristics (will) define my leadership? Why these and not others?

Each preparation program can modify the questions to suit their purposes and their students. Although people's right to pass on specific questions should be respected, further reflection will be encouraged by having students share their responses and discuss with their professors the moral demands of being authentic as a leader. A follow-up to this exercise might be having each student write out his or her own "authenticity platform," a focused expression of personal, professional, and civic authenticity. These exercises might be conducted at the beginning of the program and at the end, as a way for candidates to assess their growth in the virtue of authenticity.

• *A presence audit.* This exercise requires candidates to assess the quality of the way they are present to other people and to the conditions of their life and of their work, as well as how they exercise presence in their leadership of schools. The exercise can begin with a treatment of the ways of being present, such as affirming presence, critical presence, and enabling presence. Candidates are required to respond in their journals to questions such as the following:

1. What persons, situations, or things do you give your full attention to on any given day? Why these and not others?

2. What in nature really grabs your attention, and why? How do you feel in those moments?

3. Can you name a person who is really present to you, who gives you unconditional attention? What does that feel like, and why?

4. What aspects of your work fully engage you, drawing you into a kind of flowing dialogue? Describe how that happens.

5. What aspects of your work really frustrate you? Get up close to that experience. What is going on there? Is there a larger issue or problem underlying it? If you were in charge, how would you change this?

6. How is being present to something or someone a dialogue, a process of sending and receiving signals, messages, or feelings? Describe an experience you had that was like that.

7. Are you present to underperforming students? Do you know specifically why each one is not doing well in his or her schoolwork? Are you present to the possibilities in each underperforming student?

8. Be present to what it would take to transform your school into a more exciting place for learning. Try to name what it would take. How does that possibility challenge your authenticity as an educator? What does that possibility ask of you?

Again, while preserving people's right to pass on any given question, it is helpful for the group to share their answers and to discuss their answers to question 8. The group can be asked to design a brief weekly assessment exercise on how they experienced presence and exercised presence during the past week and possibly to do some small-group sharing of the results each week.

• A *responsibility audit*. This is an exercise in which candidates are required to respond to a variety of reflective questions about their sense of their responsibilities. Again, this exercise can be preceded by an exploration of the "do no harm" and proactive aspects of responsibility and of the different perspectives when one is seen as responsible as, responsible to, and responsible for. The exercise includes their writing responses in a journal to questions such as the following:

1. In your work, what types of harm are you responsible for preventing? How does that differ from your responsibility to prevent harm when you are acting as a citizen outside the school?

2. In your family, what are your responsibilities? What is the source of those responsibilities? Can you distinguish some superficial motives for fulfilling these responsibilities from some deeper motivations?

3. In your work, what are you responsible for promoting? How well do you do that?

4. In your work, to whom are you responsible? Explain the grounds of your responsibility in each case.

5. To whom are you responsible in your personal life? Explain the grounds of that responsibility. Where does it come from?

6. For what are you responsible in your personal life? Where does that sense of responsibility originate?

7. When are you not responsible in your personal life, and how do you know it?

8. When are you not responsible in your work, and how do you know it?

9. How do you deal with colleagues who are not responsible? Why?

10. What is the common work for which everyone in your school or organization is held responsible? Does everyone in fact exercise that responsibility well? What would be needed to have everyone exercise that responsibility well?

Again, the opportunity for candidates to share their responses prolongs and deepens their reflections, as does engaging their professors in discussing responses.

• *An audit of authentic learning.* If authentic learning is the crucial common work of the school, the cultivation of which constitutes the core of the proactive responsibilities of the educational leader, then the candidates, most or all of whom are currently or have recently been teaching in schools, can conduct an audit of their school or a school that they might have easy access to. This exercise can be carried out in one of the courses in the program or separately as a small research project. The audit should be preceded by a fairly thorough exploration of what constitutes authentic learning. The work of Fred Newmann and Associates (1996) and of Wiggins and McTighe (1998) is very helpful in this effort, but there are other meanings of "authentic learning" that need to be explored, especially when working with second-language or second-culture students, with underperforming students, and with special needs students. What qualifies learning as authentic in a given instance for a student from one of these groups might look very different from the accepted version.

In this exercise, candidates can simply be asked to identify three to five examples of what they consider authentic learning, describe them, and explain why they are indeed examples of authentic learning. Sharing these examples will generate considerable disagreement over what constitutes authentic learning, but that constitutes the very worth of the exercise, for there is no universal agreement on this topic. Professors of curriculum and of learning theory should be included in these sessions. The position that I have taken here and elsewhere (Starratt, 2003) is that authentic learning is not simply an intellectual activity but a moral activity as well, for it engages the learner in an authentic relationship with what is being learned. The learning respects the authenticity of the subject matter, as well as the authenticity of the learning process itself—and that adds a moral quality to the learning. What is learned is respected in its own right and creates a dialogue with the learner about its significance for her or him.

This exercise can be followed by a more ambitious exercise of comparing the number of authentic learning episodes observed with the number of learning episodes that do not measure up to the criteria of authenticity. This data collection can be followed by speculation about possible obstacles to authentic learning in the classroom situation and further speculation on what it would take to bring about increased authentic learning for all the students. This kind of work on the part of graduate students who are preparing to become educational leaders is essential if they are to be prepared to engage this core work of educational leadership.

With imagination, other exercises for candidates for and practitioners of school leadership can readily be designed. The point here is that this kind of direct involvement in probing the underlying moral and ethical issues in the very conduct of schooling is required for the continuing education and preparation of school leaders.

Afterword

Modernity's embrace of individual autonomy and the simultaneous displacement, for all practical purposes, of divine providence in human affairs brought to the fore an emphasis on responsibility. That is both good news and bad news. The good news is that this attitude removed the fatalistic excuse that God's will was responsible for disease, infant mortality, floods, and a host of other calamities of human history. The bad news is that we now realize that *we* are individually and collectively responsible for the world we inhabit.

That is bad news in the sense that such responsibility means that we never get a holiday from these responsibilities. Now, when we go for a family picnic along the shores of a country lake, we bring along an extra trash bag or two, knowing that we cannot throw our leftovers into the lake or under a bush. The AIDS epidemic is a stark reminder of other forms of responsibility. Cheating on our taxes is a failure to participate in our common responsibility to sustain our society's infrastructure of roads, schools, hospitals, and police protection. It is bad news in a deeper sense in that the whole world, as Crotty (2001) observes, "presents its terrible needs to us for our response. . . . The demands of responsibility are capable neither of being satisfied nor of being silenced" (pp. 118–119).

In earlier times, a belief in divine providence did not really shelter us from responsibility for our choices, but it sheltered us from the crushing finality of tragedies that befell us when forces over which we had no control wiped out our cherished dreams and actual accomplishments. Divine providence did not protect us from tragedy in this life; in the next life, however, God's justice and mercy would reward those who held steadfast. Today, for all intents and purposes, belief in divine providence has no place in public affairs. That is why the advocates for public causes (saving the whales; fighting the scourges of cancer, AIDS, and Alzheimer's disease; or preserving the forests, the water supply, and the ozone layer) sometimes seem driven by a relentless sense of responsibility and spread a sense of guilt among the less committed members of the community. As they say, if we don't do it, nothing will save us from the spread of these catastrophes.

Surely there are miles to go before the collective energies and intelligence of the human race can rest from its responsibilities to save the environment, eradicate disease, and create equitable and humane social structures that support a decent quality of life for everyone. In the meantime, bad things continue to happen to people. Those in positions of responsibility—in this book, educational leaders—have to carry the burdens of being proactively responsible for changing those things over which they have some control in order to alleviate disadvantage and promote the deeply human fulfillment of young people. But educational leaders have to live with the limitations over which they have little control. They have to live with the tragedies of thwarted human potential, diminished human dreams, and seemingly crushing handicaps that populate the corridors of their schools. I am not suggesting that educational leaders walk away from the human beings who bear such burdens. Rather, I am suggesting that leaders discover a fellowship with those people *within* the circumstances of their lives, that leaders appreciate the deep wellsprings of human possibility from which human beings can draw, achieving fulfillment even in the most desperate of circumstances. Schools should be places where everyone watches out for the ones carrying the heaviest burdens, whether those burdens appear in the form of a congenital disability, a chaotic home environment, the loss of a home to a fire or a tornado, or the loss of a parent or a sibling. We discover our own humanity in caring for others with heavier burdens than ours. Even when we can do nothing to remove those burdens, a gesture of care can lighten the burden, a word of encouragement can lead to enacting possibilities despite the burdens.

Leaders have to find a way to confront and accept the limitations of their leadership. Other people will not always be amenable to how the leader thinks they should live their lives. Students may resist school-imposed learning but nonetheless learn other important life lessons on their own, in their own time. People will walk away from the work the leader has embraced, but they will find other work in which they can make a contribution. People who never come up to the leader's expectations can nonetheless lead very satisfying lives. What the leader considers failures can sometimes lead to other results considered quite satisfying by others.

Leaders should weep over the suffering of others, especially the young. They should do what they can to alleviate suffering. But leaders cannot be defeated by their inability to right some wrongs, to bring every teacher up to peak performance, to bring every student up to a passing grade this year. They have to take responsibility for doing what they can with the resources at their disposal and recognize that their perspectives and energies are not only limited but sometimes imperfect and misplaced. They need continually to be present to both the enormous possibilities in every day and in every person and to the limitations that every person has to live with. Moral leadership cannot stand above the human condition. At the same time, moral leadership invites others to transform each day into something special, something wonderful, something unforgettable, something that enables their human spirit to soar and, giddy with the joy of the moment, know who they are.

References

Adams, J. E., & Kirst, M. W. (1999). New demands and concepts for educational accountability: Striving for results in an era of excellence. In J. Murphy & K. S. Louis (Eds.), *Handbook of research on educational administration* (2nd ed., pp. 463–489). San Francisco: Jossey-Bass.

Anton, C. (2001). *Selfhood and authenticity.* Albany: State University of New York Press.

Argyris, C. (1977). Double-loop learning in organizations. *Harvard Business Review, 55*(5), 115–125.

Ashton, P. T., & Webb, R. B. (1986). *Making a difference: Teachers' sense of efficacy and student achievement.* New York: Longman.

Auhagen, A. E., & Bierhoff, H. W. (Eds.). (2001a). *Responsibility: The many faces of a social phenomenon.* London: Routledge.

Auhagen, A. E., & Bierhoff, H. W. (2001b). Responsibility as a fundamental human phenomenon. In A. E. Auhagen & H. W. Bierhoff (Eds.), *Responsibility: The many faces of a social phenomenon* (pp. 1–8). London: Routledge.

Auhagen, A. E., & Bierhoff, H. W. (2001c). Responsibility at the beginning of the third millennium. In A. E. Auhagen & H. W. Bierhoff (Eds.), *Responsibility: The many faces of a social phenomenon* (pp. 179–184). London: Routledge.

Barber, M. (1996). *The learning game: Arguments for an education revolution.* London: Victor Gollancz.

Bateson, G. (1979). *Mind and nature: A necessary unity.* New York: Dutton.

Bauman, Z. (1995). *Life in fragments: Essays in postmodern morality*. Oxford, England: Blackwell.

Becker, E. (1971). *The birth and death of meaning* (2nd ed.). New York: Free Press.

Birnbacher, D. (2001). Philosophical foundations of responsibility. In A. E. Auhagen & H. W. Bierhoff (Eds.), *Responsibility: The many faces of a social phenomenon* (pp. 9–22). London: Routledge.

Birnbaum, D. (1998). *The hospitality of presence: Problems of otherness in Husserl's phenomenology*. Stockholm, Sweden: Almqvist & Wiskell International.

Blasé, J., & Blasé, J. (2003). *Breaking the silence: Overcoming the problem of principal mistreatment of teachers*. Thousand Oaks, CA: Corwin Press.

Bohm, D. (1981). *Wholeness and the implicate order*. London: Routledge and Kegan Paul.

Bonnet, M., & Cuypers, S. (2003). Autonomy and authenticity in education. In N. Blake, P. Smeyers, R. Smith, & P. Standish (Eds.), *The Blackwell guide to the philosophy of education* (pp. 326–340). Oxford, England: Blackwell.

Bottery, M. (2000). *Education, policy and ethics*. London: Continuum.

Brueggemann, W. (2001). Law as response to Thou. In W. Davis (Ed.), *Taking responsibility: Comparative perspectives* (pp. 87–105). Charlottesville: University Press of Virginia.

Buzzelli, C. A., & Johnston, B. (2002). *The moral dimension of teaching: Language, power, and culture in classroom interaction*. New York: Routledge Falmer.

Carnegie Council on Adolescent Development. (1989). *Turning points: Preparing youth for the 21st century*. New York: Carnegie Corporation of New York.

Cooper, T. L. (1991). *An ethic of citizenship for public administration*. Upper Saddle River, NJ: Prentice Hall.

Cooper, T. L. (1998). *The responsible administrator: An approach to ethics for the administrative role* (4th ed.). San Francisco: Jossey-Bass.

Cooper, T. L. (Ed.). (2001). *Handbook of administrative ethics* (2nd ed.). New York: Dekker.

Crotty, K. (2001). Democracy, tragedy, and responsibility. In W. Davis (Ed.), *Taking responsibility: Comparative perspectives* (pp. 106–120). Charlottesville: University Press of Virginia.

Davidson, P., & Youniss, J. (1995). Moral development and social construction. In W. M. Kurtines & J. L. Gewirtz (Eds.), *Moral development: An introduction* (pp. 289–310). Boston: Allyn & Bacon.

Davis, W. (2001). Introduction: The dimensions and dilemmas of a modern virtue. In W. Davis (Ed.), *Taking responsibility: Comparative perspectives* (pp. 1–27). Charlottesville: University Press of Virginia.

Duignan, P. (2003a, August). *Authenticity in leadership: Encouraging the heart, celebrating the spirit.* Paper presented at the National Conference of Lutheran Principles, Canberra, Australia.

Duignan, P. (2003b, September). *Formation of capable, influential, and authentic leaders for times of uncertainty.* Paper presented at the National Conference of Australian Primary Principals' Association, Adelaide.

Duignan, P., Burford, C., Cresp, M., d'Arbon, T., Fagan, M., & Frangoulis, M. (2003). Executive summary. In *Contemporary challenges and implications for leaders in frontline human service organizations.* Strathfield, NSW: The SOLAR Project, Australian Catholic University.

Eisenstadt, S. N. (Ed.). (1968). *Max Weber: Charisma and institution building.* Chicago: University of Chicago Press.

Evans, R. (1996). *The human side of school change.* San Francisco: Jossey-Bass.

Foster, W. (1986). *Paradigms and promises: New approaches to educational administration.* Buffalo, NY: Prometheus Books.

Foster, W. (2000, November). *Democracy, leadership, and the technologies of thought.* Paper presented at the annual conference of the University Council for Educational Administration, Albuquerque, NM.

Fullan, M. (2003). *The moral imperative of school leadership.* Thousand Oaks, CA: Corwin Press.

Furman, G. (2003). What is leadership for? *UCEA Review,* 55(1).

Goldring, E., & Greenfield, W. (2002). Understanding the evolving concept of leadership in education: Roles, expectations and dilemmas. In J. Murphy (Ed.), *One hundred first yearbook of the National Society for the Study of Education: Part I. The educational leadership challenge: Redefining leadership for the 21st century* (pp. 1–19). Chicago: National Society for the Study of Education.

Hargreaves, A. (2003). *Teaching in the knowledge society: Education in the age of uncertainty.* New York: Teachers College Press.

Hargreaves, A., Earl, L., Moore, S., & Manning, S. (2001). *Learning to change: Teaching beyond subjects and standards.* San Francisco: Jossey-Bass.

Heidegger, M. (1962). *Being and time.* (J. Macquarrie and E. Robinson, Trans.). New York: HarperCollins.

Heifetz, R. A. (1994). *Leadership without easy answers.* Cambridge, MA: Belknap Press of Harvard University Press.

Heifetz, R. A., & Linsky, M. (2002). *Leadership on the line: Staying alive through the dangers of leading.* Boston: Harvard Business School Press.

Hodgkinson, C. (1991). *Educational leadership: The moral art.* Albany: State University of New York Press.

Hynds, S. (1997). *On the brink: Negotiating literature and life with adolescents.* New York: Teachers College Press.

Jonsen, A. (1968). *Responsibility in modern religious ethics.* Washington, DC: Corpus Books.

Langlois, L. (2001). Les directeurs generales et les commisaires scolaires: Liaisons dangereuses? [The directors general and the school commissions: Dangerous relationships?]. *Education et Francophonie, 29*(2).

Langlois, L. (2002, October). *Ethical equilibrist practices beyond the administrative net.* Paper presented at the Seventh Annual Values and Leadership Conference, Toronto.

Langlois, L., & Starratt, R. J. (2000, November). *What we know and how we know it: Ethical decision-making of superintendents.* Paper presented at the annual conference of the University Council on Educational Administration, Albuquerque, NM.

Langlois, L., & Starratt, R. J. (2002, November). *Ethical administrative practice within postmodern complexity: An analysis of the decision-making process of Quebec superintendents*. Paper presented at the annual conference of the University Council on Educational Administration, Pittsburgh, PA.

Larson, C. L., & Murtadha, K. (2002). Leadership for social justice. In J. Murphy (Ed.), *One hundred first yearbook of the National Society for the Study of Education: Part I. The educational leadership challenge: Redefining leadership for the 21st century* (pp. 134–161). Chicago: National Society for the Study of Education.

Leithwood, K., & Prestine, N. (2002). Unpacking the challenges of leadership at the school. In J. Murphy (Ed.), *One hundred first yearbook of the National Society for the Study of Education: Part I. The educational leadership challenge: Redefining leadership for the 21st century* (pp. 42–64). Chicago: National Society for the Study of Education.

Lerner, R. (2001). The American founders' responsibility. In W. Davis (Ed.), *Taking responsibility: Comparative perspectives* (pp. 31–46). Charlottesville: University Press of Virginia.

Loader, D. N. (1997). *The inner principal*. London: Falmer Press.

Lugg, C. A., Bulkley, K., Firestone, W. A., & Garner, C. W. (2002). The contextual terrain facing educational leaders. In J. Murphy (Ed.), *One hundred first yearbook of the National Society for the Study of Education: Part I. The educational leadership challenge: Redefining leadership for the 21st century* (pp. 20–41). Chicago: National Society for the Study of Education.

Maxcy, S. J. (2002). *Ethical school leadership*. Lanham, MD: Scarecrow Press.

Mead, G. H. (1934). *Mind, self and society*. Chicago: University of Chicago Press.

Meier, D. (1998). Authenticity and educational change. In A. Hargreaves, A. Lieberman, M. Fullan, & D. Hopkins (Eds.). *International handbook of educational change* (pp. 596–615). London: Kluwer.

Moran, G. (1996). *A grammar of responsibility*. New York: Crossroads.

Newmann, F. M., & Associates. (1996). *Authentic achievement: Restructuring schools for intellectual quality*. San Francisco: Jossey-Bass.

Niebuhr, R. (1963). *The responsible self: An essay in Christian moral philosophy*. New York: HarperCollins.

Noddings, N. (1992). *The challenge to care in schools: An alternative approach to education*. New York: Teachers College Press.

Oakes, J., Quartz, K. H., Ryan, S., & Lipton, M. (2000). *Becoming good American schools: The struggle for civic virtue in educational reform*. San Francisco: Jossey-Bass.

Senge, P. (1990). *The fifth discipline*. New York: Doubleday.

Sergiovanni, T. J. (1992). *Moral leadership: Getting to the heart of school improvement*. San Francisco: Jossey-Bass.

Sergiovanni, T. J., & Starratt, R. J. (2002). *Supervision: A redefinition* (7th ed.). New York: McGraw-Hill.

Shapiro, J. P., & Stefkovich, J. A. (2001). *Ethical leadership and decision making in education: Applying theoretical perspectives to complex dilemmas*. Mahwah, NJ: Erlbaum.

Starratt, R. J. (1991). Building an ethical school: A theory for practice in educational leadership. *Educational Administration Quarterly, 27*(2), 185–202.

Starratt, R. J. (1994). *Building an ethical school: A practical response to the moral crisis in schools*. London: Falmer Press.

Starratt, R. J. (2003). *Centering educational administration: Cultivating meaning, community, and responsibility*. Mahwah, NJ: Erlbaum.

Strike, K. A., Haller, E. J., & Soltis, J. F. (1998). *The ethics of school administration* (2nd ed.). New York: Teachers College Press.

Taylor, C. (1991). *The ethics of authenticity*. Cambridge, MA: Harvard University Press.

Vogel, L. (2001). Jewish philosophies after Heidegger: Levinas and Jonas on responsibility. In W. Davis (Ed.), *Taking responsibility: Comparative perspectives* (pp. 121–146). Charlottesville: University Press of Virginia.

Weber, M. (1958). The Protestant sects and the spirit of capitalism. In H. H. Gerth & C. W. Mills (Eds.), *From Max Weber: Essays in sociology* (pp. 302–332). New York: Oxford University Press.

Wiggins, G., & McTighe, J. (1998). *Understanding by design*. Alexandria, VA: Association for Supervision and Curriculum Development.

Wiles, M. (1983). *Children into pupils*. London: Routledge and
    Kegan Paul.
Youniss, J. (1981). An analysis of moral development through a
    theory of social construction. *Merrill-Palmer Quarterly, 27,*
    385–403.

Index